THE DEATH OF THE
USS *THRESHER*

THE DEATH OF THE USS *THRESHER*

Norman Polmar

The Lyons Press

Guilford, Connecticut

An imprint of The Globe Pequot Press

To the Officers and Enlisted Men of the United States Ship
Thresher, who went to sea in her on April 9, 1963,
and
John Slinkman, my editor, mentor, and friend,
who told me to write about the *Thresher.*

CONTENTS

"The man who ventures to write contemporary history must expect to be criticized both for everything he has said and everything he has not said."

—Voltaire
in a letter to M. Bertin de Rocheret

PREFACE

In the eerie pre-dawn light of an April morning, a huge black shape rested in the waters that washed the shores of Portsmouth, New Hampshire. Clustered on that shore were scores of buildings that, less than two years before, had been the birthplace of the black mass of steel that now lay tethered to the shore by steel cables and a wooden pier.

Before the first rays of sunlight touched down on the black submarine or the nearby buildings, a strange light began to glow deep in the bowels of the submarine. Inside the lead-lined reactor, nuclear fission—the same power that fired the sun—fired a maze of machinery inside the strange craft. Human beings—more than one hundred of them—turned valves and threw switches that seemingly brought the black shape to life. Thus the USS *Thresher* came alive on the morning of April 9, 1963.

The men of the submarine's anchor detail cast off the steel cables that tied her to shore and slowly headed down river and into the great ocean beyond. On the bridge atop the submarine's sail structure a young officer carefully surveyed the ship he commanded. He listened with confidence to the sounds of the men working inside his ship and the sounds of water rushing by the ship's hull.

The ship was the most advanced attack nuclear submarine ever built. Her sonar could probe out enemy submarines at greater distances than ever before. The new torpedo-missile weapon system planned for her would kill enemy submarines faster and at greater distances than ever before. The *Thresher* herself was ultra-silent when operating in the depths, making her relatively immune to enemy detection devices. And the *Thresher*, by operating in depths far beyond the reach of most enemy weapons, would be shrouded in a mantle of immunity. Nine months in the Portsmouth Naval Shipyard had tuned up the *Thresher*, eliminating what "bugs" had been found in her design and construction.

On April 9 the *Thresher* made a successful dive to relatively shallow depths in the waters off New England. She then headed out to deep water for a dive to her maximum operating or test depth. On the morning of April 10 she slowly descended. Some 40 times before she had gone down to such a depth and returned safely.

This time the *Thresher* did not return to the surface.

The *Thresher*—and the 129 men in her—died on the morning of April 10. It was the worst submarine disaster to that time. In the ensuing decades no fewer than six additional nuclear submarines would be lost at sea, one American, the USS *Scorpion*, and five Soviet-Russian. But the *Thresher* would remain the most tragic sinking in number of men killed, and she would have the dubious distinction of being the first nuclear submarine to be lost.

This book is the story of the *Thresher*, her beginning, her short career, and her death. It is the story of a magnificent submarine, an outstanding crew, and the worst submarine disaster in history.

The description of what went on inside the *Thresher* during her final hours is drawn together from men who were intimately familiar with the *Thresher* and men who earlier sailed in her. Indeed, the commanding officer who took the *Thresher* down on her first dive to test depth—and halted the dive because of the possibility that the *Thresher* was diving to disaster—has been kind enough to help me with this project. He and the others who contributed to this book are listed in the acknowledgments.

Submarines are known by many terms—some flattering, some not so. Traditionally they are called "boats." In the nuclear age their size and cost almost dictates that they be properly labeled "ships." The terms are used interchangeably by submariners and I use them here as they were spoken and written.

—Norman Polmar

ACKNOWLEDGMENTS

This book was originally written because of Thomas B. Allen, then managing editor of Chilton Books, which published the first edition of *Death of the Thresher* in 1964. Mr. Allen and I subsequently have collaborated in writing seven books and numerous articles.

The original book was written with the extensive help of many individuals, but especially Captain Dominic A. Paolucci, one of the Navy's outstanding submariners. He was a 1943 graduate of the Naval Academy and held the degree of Doctor of Philosophy in mathematics from Indiana University. Captain Paolucci was most familiar with *Thresher*-class submarines: From 1958 to 1961 he was head of the submarine training and policy section in the Office of the Chief of Naval Operations; from 1961 to 1963 he helped plan the integration of *Thresher*-class submarines into the Pacific Fleet while on the staff of the Commander, Submarine Force, Pacific Fleet; in July, 1963 he took command of Submarine Division 71, consisting of five nuclear-powered submarines, two of them sisters to the *Thresher*. Following his retirement from the Navy in 1969 he and I worked together in the corporate world for ten years.

I was also greatly in debt to Rear Admiral Dean L. Axene, the first commanding officer of the *Thresher*, and to Rear

Admiral David M. Cooney, at the time head of the magazine and book section of Navy Information. Both contributed much time and effort to this project.

In writing the original book, Dr. Arthur E. Maxwell of the Office of Naval Research aided in writing about the search phase of the *Thresher* story; Lieutenant Commander Don Keach, former skipper of the bathyscaph *Trieste*, provided details of his dives in search of the *Thresher*; Commander John H. Nicholson, a veteran nuclear submariner, helped with technical details of the *Thresher*; Captain Tazewell T. Shepard Jr., former Naval Aide to the President, described events at the White House on April 10, 1963; Captain H. B. Sweitzer, former aide to the Vice Chief of Naval Operations, provided details of the events in the Pentagon on April 10, 1963; Commander Howard N. Larcombe, commanding officer of the USS *Dogfish*, furnished details of the *Thresher*'s departure on her last cruise; and Lieutenants Don Walsh and Lawrence Shumaker, the first Navymen assigned to the bathyscaph *Trieste*, "educated" me in her ways.

The Office of Navy Information was been most cooperative, especially Lieutenant Commanders Frederick A. Prehn and Frank Steele, and Anthony Metro, yeoman second class. Lieutenant Richard Green and Robert L. Wilkie, master chief yeoman, of the Bureau of Naval Personnel, were also most helpful.

From 1967 to 1970, while an employee of the Northrop Corporation, I had the privilege of working directly for the Navy's Deep Submergence Systems Project, initially headed by Dr. John P. Craven and then Captain William Nicholson. I was given a unique opportunity to learn about DSSP's programs from them and, especially Captain George Bond, the "father" of saturation diving; Commander Scott Carpenter, astronaut-aquanaut; Lieutenant Harris Steinke; and many other members of the technical staff.

The many hours of time spent on this book by my wife, Beverly, and the late Mrs. "Daly" Paolucci greatly contributed to this work.

CHAPTER 1

THE *THRESHER*

From her very beginning the *Thresher* was to have had a special place in naval history. In the nuclear-missile age, the missile-firing submarine was the most deadly weapon system in existence. The missile-firing, nuclear-propelled submarine, steaming slowly in the depths of the ocean, was seemingly invulnerable to almost all methods of detection and destruction. As nuclear submarine technology advanced in the late 1950s, it soon became apparent that the best way to kill such a craft was with another nuclear-propelled submarine.

Thus, in the 1960's the leading maritime nations—the United States, Great Britain, France, and the Soviet Union—began building fleets of missile-firing submarines. And, to protect their own cities and military installations from the devastation of enemy missile submarines, each nation began building a fleet of hunter-killer submarines.

In the United States Navy, the "ultimate" hunter-killer submarine was the *Thresher*. Sixty years of submarine technology, the experience of two world wars, and the knowledge obtained by leading the world in nuclear power development went into the *Thresher's* design.

The Navy's top submariners and engineers planned the *Thresher*. She would combine within a single, high-speed hull the most advanced sonar in existence to detect enemy submarines; special silencing features that would make her very hard to find; advanced weapons that could strike out and destroy an enemy submarine many miles away; high submerged speed that could quickly bring her within striking range of enemy submarines; and the ability to operate at depths deeper than any previous submarine could go. This last feature would be of particular importance: The deeper submarines can dive, the more difficult they are to detect and destroy; the faster submarines can go, the more important it is for them to have more "maneuvering room" to take full advantage of their speed and agility with a margin of safety. And there are indications that at very deep depths there are underwater "sound channels" that may greatly increase the range of sonar in deep-diving submarines. Because the enemy would also try to build deep-diving submarines, the deeper a hunter-killer submarine could operate, the more chance of success she would have against advanced enemy undersea craft.

To make the *Thresher* able to withstand the intense pressure at deeper depths the Navy could either increase the thickness of her hull or use a stronger steel. Using thicker steel would be difficult because of problems in making reliable welds in the thicker metal. For the *Thresher* the Navy decided to use stronger steel—the so-called HY-80 steel which could withstand the pressure of 80,000 pounds per square inch before it would start pulling apart. With a submarine hull built for deeper operation the Navy would get a bonus with the *Thresher*. Because of her hull strength, in shallow waters she would be able to withstand greater shocks from enemy weapons.

The decision to go deep was controversial. Captain Donald Kern, head of preliminary design in the Bureau of Ships, later recalled the views of Admiral Hyman G. Rickover, head of the Navy's nuclear propulsion program: "He wanted no part of the deep diving. He thought we were wasting our time and that this was foolish going to the deeper depth, and he fought that tooth and nail, too. I had knock-down, drag-out battles with him on that."

While the *Thresher* was under construction, the following exchange occurred between Admiral Rickover and Representative George Mahon, a member of the House Appropriations Committee:

Mahon. Are you over-designing these ships? I am talking now mostly about submarines. Are you putting on refinements that are really not necessary? You spoke of the *Thresher* diving to a very great depth.

Rickover. Yes, sir.

Mahon. How deep are you going?

Rickover. The World War II submarines were designed for [400] feet. Right after World War II we developed the present [750]-foot submarines. Now we are going to [1,300] feet. The reason is that the deeper a ship goes, the less it is possible to detect it. It can take advantage of various thermal layers in the ocean. It also is less susceptible to damage by various types of depth charges and other anti-submarine devices. The greater depth gives it greater invisibility, greater invulnerability. We would like to go deeper if we could, but a point comes where existing hull steel may not be able safely to withstand the greater pressure. . . . However, there is considerable military advantage, Mr. Mahon, to be able to go deeper; it is somewhat analogous to having airplanes which can fly higher

Although not specifically designed for high speed, the *Thresher* would be able to move as fast underwater as any other U.S. submarine except for the near-contemporary *Skipjack*-class nuclear submarines. But speed would be of secondary importance to the *Thresher*. Her primary assignment would be to cruise slowly—hence silently—off enemy ports or in narrow waterways to catch and kill enemy submarines en route to attack friendly shipping or cities. Alternatively, if she could be initially guided to an enemy submarine by an "external" source, the *Thresher* could hopefully trail the hostile craft, collecting intelligence on the submarine or standing ready to attack. While designed primarily to hunt and kill enemy submarines, the *Thresher* would also be able to attack surface warships and merchantmen, a mission of submarines since they were first conceived.

Like her nuclear-propelled predecessors, the *Thresher* was designed to spend most of her time operating in the depths of the seas. Thus she was designed with a modified spindle, or cigar-shaped hull, that is most efficient underwater, derived from the U.S. experimental submarine *Albacore*. At one point it was proposed to delete the superstructure or "sail" from the *Thresher*, a radical departure from traditional submarine designs. However, a small sail structure was provided, albeit as small as possible to reduce the craft's underwater "drag." This would make her faster and quieter. To give her the smallest sail area possible the *Thresher* would not have a mast fitted with the intelligence collection antennas found in contemporary submarines, and certain other equipment was deleted.

Mounted on each side of the *Thresher*'s sail would be her diving planes. These small, wing-like devices, coupled with stern diving planes, would guide the submarine up and down through the water. On most earlier submarines the forward diving planes are found at the bow. Mounting them on the *Thresher*'s sail would move the turbulence they created as far as possible from the submarine's bow sonar, thus reducing acoustic interference to the craft's all-important "ears."

Internally the *Thresher* would also be an unusual submarine. Other submarines—with the lone exception of the contemporary nuclear-propelled *Tullibee*—had their sonar equipment fitted where space could be found. On the drawing boards the submarine's torpedo tubes, torpedoes, controls, machinery, and living accommodations were usually carefully laid out. Then the sonar was fitted in. Not so with the *Thresher,* which would be designed around her sonar equipment. This new sonar system or "suit" would be in her bow, traditional location of a submarine's torpedo tubes. The bow position was the most advantageous, for it placed the sonar as far as possible from the noise-interference of the craft's machinery and propeller. The *Thresher's* sonar would be the most advanced submarine listening device yet built. The first such set—designated AN/BQQ-2—was fitted in the nuclear submarine *Tullibee.* It could detect the sounds made by other submarines at greater distances than any previous submarine sonar.

The *Thresher's* four torpedo tubes would be farther back in her hull, angled out, two to each side, at ten degrees from the centerline. They would be able to fire conventional anti-shipping or anti-submarine torpedoes (including wire-guided torpedoes) and the Mk 45 ASTOR (Anti-Submarine Torpedo), a wire-guided weapon that carried a nuclear warhead. Later the *Thresher* would be fitted with the SUBROC (Submarine Rocket), a weapon launched from a torpedo tube like a conventional torpedo, but then streak up to the surface, leave the water in a ballistic trajectory, and then plunge back into the water several miles from the *Thresher.* After reentering the water, SUBROC's nuclear warhead would detonate. Including weapons in the four torpedo tubes, the *Thresher* would carry about 25 weapons—torpedoes, SUBROCs, and tube-launched sea mines.

To drive the *Thresher* through the depths she would have an S5W nuclear reactor. This was already the workhorse of the United States nuclear submarine fleet and was used in Britain's first nuclear submarine, HMS *Dreadnought*. The S5W reactors powered the *Thresher*'s predecessors of the *Skipjack* class and all 41 U.S. Polaris missile submarines. The reactor would produce steam that would turn a turbine to drive the submarine's single propeller. Nuclear power also would provide virtually limitless fresh water, long considered a luxury in non-nuclear submarines, as well as air conditioning, vital for the mass of electronic equipment in the craft as well as for crew comfort. For emergency use—and to provide electricity in port when the atomic plant would be shut down—the *Thresher* would also have a small diesel-electric power plant.

Nine officers and 95 enlisted men would normally operate the *Thresher*—some 20 more than were found in U.S. submarines in World War II, but still some 30 fewer men than the number needed to operate a Polaris missile submarine.

Even the construction of the *Thresher* would be unusual. The lead ships for all earlier classes of United States nuclear submarines, the *Nautilus, Seawolf, Skate, Skipjack, Tullibee,* and *George Washington,* were built at the commercial Electric Board yard in Groton, Connecticut. The *Thresher* would be built in the government-operated Portsmouth Naval Shipyard, located on Kittery Island in Maine.

The first hull sections of the *Thresher*—her keel laying— were put in place on the building way at Portsmouth on May 28, 1958. Slowly she took shape. From her blunt bow to her propeller-tipped stern the *Thresher* would measure 278 feet, 6 inches. Her almost circular hull would be 31 feet, 8 inches at its widest point. The *Thresher* was shorter and fatter than her World War II ancestors because of her *Albacore* hull design. This would give her a greater "volume" and hence more displacement—just over 3,500 tons on the surface compared to just under 1,600 tons for World War II submarines.

With emphasis being given to the Polaris missile submarine program from the late 1950s onward, construction of the *Thresher* lagged slightly, and she was on the building ways for almost two years. (A prototype Polaris submarine built at the same time was on the ways only 14 months.)

The *Thresher* was launched on July 9, 1960, with Mrs. Mary B. Warder smashing the traditional bottle of champagne against the submarine. In doing so she formally named the steel hull *Thresher*. The submarine's name honored a World War II-era undersea craft that had been a top scorer against Japanese merchantmen in the Pacific. She in turn had been named for the long-tailed *Thresher* shark. As Mrs. Warder, wife of Rear Admiral Frederick B. Warder, a veteran submariner, christened her, the black hull that was now the *Thresher* began to slide into the waters of the Piscataqua River. Because of her size and design, the *Thresher* slid into the water bow first, the first U.S. submarine to be launched in that fashion. The last U.S. warships to be launched bow first were scout cruisers built some 40 years earlier.

The *Thresher*'s first "cruise" was brief, for, as she became completely waterborne, special chains and lines slowed her to a stop. Then tug boats eased her to a nearby dock. There workers swarmed over her. More than a year's work still remained to be done before the *Thresher* would be ready for sea.

Since she was not yet a commissioned unit of the fleet, the *Thresher* officially had no commanding officer. But for all intents and purposes she already had her "skipper": Commander

Dean L. Axene, who held orders as her "prospective" commanding officer. Born in 1923, Commander Axene entered the Naval Academy in the summer of 1941 while the United States was still officially at peace. As major battles of World War II were raging, he completed the accelerated three-year course at Annapolis. Although slight of build, he played junior varsity football all three years in school. After graduation in 1944 he was ordered to one month of indoctrination as a naval aviation observer.

But young Axene did not want to fly. He wanted to go into submarines. After attending submarine school at New London, Connecticut, he was ordered to Pearl Harbor and the submarine *Parche*. He made two war patrols into Japanese waters in the *Parche* before the war ended.

After the war, Axene studied electrical engineering at the Massachusetts Institute of Technology, saw service on submarine staffs, and aboard the submarines *Tiru* and *Sea Robin*. When Axene joined the *Sea Robin* as executive officer in June 1952, he met an ambitious junior officer then serving aboard the submarine. He was John Wesley Harvey.

From the USS *Sea Robin,* both Axene and Harvey were ordered, at different times, to be interviewed by the irascible Rear Admiral Hyman G. Rickover, head of the Navy's nuclear propulsion program. With Rickover's acquiescence, the two officers entered his training program. First Axene was ordered to the Atomic Energy Commission's Bettis Laboratory in Pittsburgh, Pennsylvania. There, and in Arco, Idaho, Axene studied nuclear propulsion. At Arco a portion of a submarine's hull had been built in a large, 385,000-gallon water tank, and inside the hull a full-size nuclear power plant, similar to that which would go to sea in a submarine, was assembled. The nuclear plant, which started up for the first time in March

1953, was used as both an engineering development model and to train naval personnel.

On September 30, 1954, Axene stood on the deck of the pioneer nuclear-propelled submarine *Nautilus* when she was placed in commission. The *Nautilus* was the world's first "vehicle" to be propelled by nuclear energy. Axene served as executive officer of the *Nautilus* until August, 1955. Just before he left the *Nautilus*, Axene welcomed aboard the submarine's new reactor officer, John Wesley Harvey.

From the *Nautilus*, Axene went on to his first command, the diesel-electric submarine *Croaker*. After the *Croaker* he became director of the nuclear department at the Navy's submarine school in New London, and then began preparation for command of the *Thresher*.

In April 1961, the *Thresher* was ready for sea. For almost a year Commander Axene had watched the *Thresher* being completed. He watched her being put together and knew her well. He was satisfied with his ship and on April 30 he took her to sea for her initial cruise. In addition to her regular crew, the *Thresher* had some 40 "riders" on board. Led by Vice Admiral Rickover, the passengers included officials and technicians from the Bureau of Ships in Washington, the Portsmouth Naval Shipyard, civilian firms with special equipment in the *Thresher*, and the submarine force staffs.

Once clear of the coast, but still over the continental shelf where the water is less than 600 feet deep, the *Thresher* made her first dive—a shallow one to check the submarine's trim and submerged control. Then she made a deeper dive in the same area. During these test dives the submarine rescue ship *Skylark* stood by on the surface to serve as a communications link and render assistance if the submarine encountered any difficulties. Since everything was normal, Commander Axene decided to undertake the deep-water dive scheduled for the next morning. The *Thresher* ran east during the night, heading for the deeper waters beyond the continental shelf.

Early on the 31st the *Thresher* began submerging into the depths. On the surface the rescue ship stood by, providing the *Thresher* with navigation checks. But should the *Thresher* run into trouble in the deep waters beyond the continental shelf there was no way of helping her. Slowly the *Thresher* went deeper and deeper, crewmen carefully checking instruments and equipment as she did so. All seemed to be going well. Then—although she was nowhere near her designed test depth of 1,300 feet—the submarine's instruments gave indications that the *Thresher* was approaching the limit of the pressure her hull could withstand. The submarine technicians on the *Thresher* were confident that the instruments, especially installed for the first deep dive, were incorrect and that everything was all right.

Axene would take no chances. Axene, who bore sole responsibility for the $45 million submarine and all of the lives in her, ordered the dive halted. Slowly the *Thresher* returned to the near-surface and headed back to Portsmouth.

Back in the shipyard, the instruments in the *Thresher* were checked and found to be incorrect. The special instrumentation was modified and the *Thresher* returned to sea to complete her trials without further incident.

The *Thresher* was now ready for service.

CHAPTER 2

A BRIEF CAREER

While a band blasted forth with rousing Sousa marches, the USS *Thresher* was commissioned in formal ceremonies at the Portsmouth Naval Shipyard on August 3, 1961. Vice Admiral Harold T. Deutermann, chief of staff to the commander of U.S. and North Atlantic Treaty Organization (NATO) forces in the Atlantic, was the principal speaker. Telling of the importance of the new submarine, he said:

> Today, as we commission *Thresher,* and make her officially a part of the Atlantic Fleet, we reach a point in submarine development long awaited by our Navy.
>
> *Thresher* is not just a new nuclear submarine, she is not just one more SSN to add to the too few that are already members of our fleets.
>
> She is not just another ship. *Thresher* is totally different!

Admiral Deutermann went on to extol the technological features brought together in the *Thresher.* But he also stressed the importance of the *Thresher*'s crew:

> Captain Axene—even though I am sure you are well aware of the fact—technology is an excellent servant, but can never be a master. . . . There will

always be technical frontiers to conquer, and we are thankful for this challenge to life, but transcending them all, is man who has the will and power to plan, to venture, and to dare.

The *Thresher* was a great scientific advancement and her crew was carefully chosen to be her master. The submarine was turned over to Commander Axene who, resplendent in his dress white uniform, read his orders placing him in command of the remarkable new warship.

To the strains of "The Star-Spangled Banner," the American flag was raised on the short flagstaff on the *Thresher's* deck. The narrow, red-white-and-blue pennant with seven stars that symbolized the ship was in commission in the U.S. Navy and under the command of an officer was raised on the short "pigstick" at the after end of the submarine's sail.

"Set the watch," ordered Commander Axene, and his executive officer, Lieutenant Commander Robert D. Rawlins, ordered the in-port watches to their stations. A reception ashore followed and soon after the crowd dispersed, the *Thresher's* crew returned to the job of loading the submarine for operations at sea.

The *Thresher's* first assignment took her south, to the Tongue of the Ocean. The "Tongue" is the deep passage north of Andros Island in the Bahama Islands. There careful studies were made of the *Thresher* to determine how much noise her machinery generated and how much sound was produced by her streamlined hull passing through water. The *Thresher* proved to be even quieter than she had been designed to be. These tests and those that followed would be the *Thresher's* "shakedown," a period of adjustment and training. For the submarine it would determine how well she met her predicted characteristics. For the crew it would prove the compatibility between man and machine.

While the *Thresher* was in the Bahamas, she was visited by Vice Admiral Elton W. Grenfell, commander of the Atlantic Fleet's Submarine Force, and Vice Admiral Edmund B. Taylor, commander of the Atlantic Fleet's Anti-Submarine Warfare Force. Both admirals had an important interest in the *Thresher*. Both flag officers were pleased with what they saw.

From the Bahamas, the *Thresher* steamed back north to the waters off New England for brief exercises. Then the *Thresher* headed for the Navy's weapons center at Newport, Rhode Island. There, during the last days of August and early September, the *Thresher* underwent her torpedo tube acceptance trials. These mated the *Thresher* to the various types of torpedoes in the Navy's arsenal.

Next, the *Thresher* took to the depths in an exercise against other submarines. In the waters off New London she played hide and seek with the nuclear-propelled undersea craft *Skate* and *Tullibee*. Interspersed with the *Thresher*'s numerous trials during her shakedown would be a series of brief in-port periods to allow for routine maintenance of equipment and rest for the submarine's crew. Normally the *Thresher* would have spent these periods in New London, her home port. However, most of the crew's families were still living in the Portsmouth area, where they had been while the submarine was under construction. Commander Axene specifically requested that the *Thresher*'s in-port upkeep be changed from New London to Portsmouth. Later, when the *Thresher* went to sea on operational missions, there would be little enough time with the families. Thus the *Thresher* tied up again at the Portsmouth Naval Shipyard.

In late October 1961 the *Thresher* went back to sea. Off Cape Cod, Massachusetts, she rendezvoused with the diesel-electric submarine *Cavalla*. Now the *Thresher* would take a "leisurely" cruise to shake down her various systems, work out, or at least find, any "bugs," and give her crew a chance to go through almost every possible maneuver. The cruise would be "leisurely" only in that it was taking the *Thresher* three weeks to travel from Portsmouth to San Juan, Puerto Rico. If she were in a hurry, she would traverse the 1,700 nautical miles in two or three days. There would be little leisure for the *Thresher*'s officers and enlisted men, who would work around the clock in underwater "games" with the *Cavalla*. The diesel-electric sub would be a "playmate" for the *Thresher*, giving the nuclear sub an opportunity to work out tactics for detecting, tracking, and attacking other submarines.

On the morning of November 2 the *Thresher* eased into historic San Juan, the capital and chief port of Puerto Rico, where her crew would get a few days of liberty. As is customary when in port, the *Thresher* shut down her nuclear reactor. When tied up in port, nuclear submarines usually used shore electrical power brought aboard by cable. But because no such power was available in San Juan, the *Thresher* started up her auxiliary diesel generator to provide "housekeeping" power for lights, air conditioning, radios, and instrumentation.

Some seven or eight hours after the reactor shutdown the diesel broke down, the result, it was later learned, of a broken pump shaft. The submarine's duty section did not immediately realize the seriousness of what had happened, and at first suspected a closed salt water cooling system—something that could be quickly repaired.

While some men worked at getting the diesel engine going again, the submarine began taking electricity from her third power source, her large electric storage battery. But the battery was limited and could not provide power for long. As it became evident that the diesel could not be quickly repaired, preparations were made to restart the submarine's nuclear power plant. But starting up a nuclear reactor is a process that takes several hours and requires large amounts of electricity.

The decision to restart the reactor was not made soon enough, and before it could be brought to the self-sustaining reaction condition, the *Thresher*'s storage battery was being rapidly depleted. What electricity could be drawn from the *Thresher*'s batteries was used in the effort to get the reactor started up and to keep vital instruments in the submarine working. Without instruments the submarine would be unable function. There was no electricity to spare for lights or ventilation.

Slowly the temperature in the submarine began going up. The reactor—a form of steam boiler—keeps its heat for many hours. This, coupled with the closed confines of the *Thresher* and the warm Caribbean night, sent the temperature inside the *Thresher*'s engine spaces soaring—90 degrees . . . 100 degrees . . . 110 degrees . . . and on up to approximately 140 degrees. To the men working inside those spaces, it felt as it the submarine had plunged into hell itself.

But the men kept working, trying to get the diesel fixed and the reactor started up. Four men would later receive Navy Commendation Medals for their work that night: Donald E. Wise, chief machinist's mate; Paul R. Tobler, electronics technician first class; Ralph W. Gould, engineman first class; and John J. Alaimo, electrician's mate first class. Wise's commendation told how "Although conditions in the engineering spaces were almost unbearable because of the extreme heat and the irritants in the air, Wise steadfastly refused to be relieved from his post throughout the entire period, and remained until he was ordered to leave the ship to receive medical attention. As soon as he was able, he returned to the engineering control station and rendered valuable assistance until again ordered to leave for his own safety."

For some ten hours there was no power but plenty of heat inside the *Thresher*. Commander Axene and others who had been ashore returned to the *Thresher* just after the submarine's battery ran down, ending the last chance of independently recovering power. He was worried about the high temperature and humidity inside the *Thresher* damaging electrical equipment, and it was becoming impossible for men to work inside the submarine.

The *Cavalla* was moored alongside the *Thresher*. Electrical cables, borrowed from another nearby ship, were connected between the *Thresher* and *Cavalla*. Then the conventional submarine started up her diesel engines to provide electrical power for the disabled *Thresher*.

Soon the *Cavalla's* electricity allowed the *Thresher* to start up her reactor and turn on lights and air conditioning. Conditions slowly returned to normal. "We could have gone to sea at six the next morning without any trouble," Commander Axene said later. During the ten hours that the *Thresher* lay in agony with little or no electricity there had been no danger of an explosion of the submarine's nuclear power plant or of radiation escaping from it. After a submarine nuclear power plant closes down, the cooling system must continue working. Although the *Thresher* had little enough electricity for this, there was always an "ace in the hole." This is an emergency cooling system using natural convection. But Commander Axene was reluctant to use this because it would mean losing the heat remaining in the reactor plant. Conservation of this heat would reduce the time needed to get the submarine's turbine-driven electrical generator working.

Since the *Thresher* had suffered no damage other than the broken-down diesel generator, which was repaired during the night, the submarine remained at San Juan to give the crew liberty. "However, the shore leave was cut for all of us, especially me, because of the 'cleaning up' job aboard the *Thresher*," Commander Axene recalled later.

From San Juan the *Thresher* steamed north again to Cape Canaveral, Florida. There she underwent additional trials and then turned back south to scenic Fort Lauderdale, Florida. At the Naval Ordnance Laboratory Test Facility there, the *Thresher* took aboard dummy SUBROC missiles. These were instrumented devices the same size and shape as the actual SUBROC missiles, but without either propellant or warhead. The *Thresher* launched these dummies as ordinance experts and *Thresher* crewmen tested the compatibility of the SUBROC and the submarine's four torpedo tubes. Like conventional torpedoes, the SUBROC missiles were ejected from the tubes with compressed air, and this system was also checked.

With Christmas coming, the *Thresher* headed back to Portsmouth. Another yard period was scheduled for the submarine, and this gave her crew some time to spend with their families. The *Thresher* had been scheduled to spend this time at New London, but Commander Axene once again prevailed upon his superiors to make it Portsmouth. Later, these extra days at home would be greatly cherished by the families of those who died in the *Thresher*.

At Portsmouth routine maintenance jobs were performed on the *Thresher*, and some modifications were made to her. Normally, after the first two or three months at sea, a new nuclear submarine goes into the yard for what is known as "post-shakedown availability." This is like the 1,000-mile checkup on a new automobile to correct minor problems and tune her up. Thus it was more than time for the *Thresher*'s "PSA." But Commander Axene didn't want to bring her in yet. "The *Thresher* had been so tied up with special tests and exercises that we had not really had a good opportunity to evaluate the ship operationally," he said. "Therefore, I asked that the extensive yard availability be delayed at least a year so we could really see what the *Thresher* could do and what 'tuning up' she needed." Again, the Navy agreed with the *Thresher*'s skipper, and maintenance that could not be delayed was performed in the brief in-port periods at Portsmouth.

The new year found the *Thresher* tied up snugly to a pier at the Portsmouth Naval Shipyard. By early February 1962, she was ready to go back to sea again for the seemingly endless tests, trials, and exercises the Navy had planned for her. The *Thresher* was new and different, and it seemed as if everybody in the Navy wanted to see what she could do in his own area of specialized interest.

Next came tests of the *Thresher*'s AN/BBQ-2 sonar suit off New London in conjunction with the Navy Underwater Sound Laboratory there. For almost three weeks she tested her advanced sonar equipment as technicians and specialists looked on. Then there was another exercise with other submarines. This time the *Thresher* again was pitted with and against the diesel-electric boats *Cavalla* and *Hardhead*.

The calendar slipped into April, and the *Thresher*, with less than one year to live, took to sea a special anti-submarine warfare study group. Inside the *Thresher* as she cruised in the depths of the Atlantic, the Navy's top military and civilian anti-submarine experts held conferences and watched the *Thresher* demonstrate her capabilities against her old companion and playmate, the *Cavalla*.

After the anti-sub experts departed, the *Thresher* took aboard Captain Frank A. Andrews, commander of Submarine Development Group 2, and his staff. They represented the *Thresher*'s parent organization. Normally submarines are assigned to squadrons, but, because the *Thresher* was new and different, she was placed under the command of this research and experimental unit.

The destination of the *Thresher* was now Charleston, South Carolina, and the naval base there that served as home for many of the nation's submarines. There local civic leaders were taken aboard for a one-day cruise to demonstrate her abilities. Soon after, the *Thresher* took part in the rehearsal for President John F. Kennedy's review of the fleet. However, the *Thresher* and several other submarines were cancelled out of the review before it was held.

Then the *Thresher* went back to Charleston to embark a group of newspaper representatives and again show what she could do. (On these guest cruises, instruments that could reveal the *Thresher*'s capabilities and some of her secret equipment were carefully covered over. Her engineering spaces were closed to all except specially authorized personnel.)

At sea again, the *Thresher* turned north for the Electric Board yard in Groton, Connecticut where she would prepare for tests that would determine how much explosive shock her hull could sustain. From earlier shock tests with other submarines technicians it was determined that some equipment in the *Thresher* would have to be modified. This work was done at Groton from April 17 to May 18. In addition, extensive instrumentation was installed in the *Thresher* to record the effects of the tests. Her entire dry food storeroom was filled with instruments; other test gadgets found their way into almost every compartment. Special movie cameras were set up to record the effects of the shock tests on selected items of equipment.

In Washington, D.C. on the morning of April 23, while the *Thresher* was at the Electric Boat Yard, Secretary of the Navy Fred Korth decorated ten engineers for their contributions to its development. Five Navy officers, ranging in rank from commander to rear admiral, were each presented a Legion of Merit award, while five civilian engineers were given Distinguished Civilian Service Awards. Four days later, in special ceremonies at the Massachusetts Institute of Technology, two additional Navy officers—both captains—were awarded Navy Commendation Medals for their roles in the design and construction of the *Thresher*. In the Navy's judgment all had done a good job on the *Thresher*.

En route to the shock tests—which would be conducted off Key West, Florida—the *Thresher* was to make two brief stops. Again she put into Fort Lauderdale and took aboard and launched SUBROC dummies.

The *Thresher's* next stop was Cape Canaveral. Her reason for going there was top secret and few would have known she even visited the port except for an "incident" that put news of the submarine in almost every newspaper in the country. At Canaveral on June 3, a tugboat—one of two coming alongside to push the *Thresher* into her berth—smashed into the low-lying submarine. The tug ripped a three-foot gash in the *Thresher's* port side, below her waterline. The hole was in a ballast tank, outside of the submarine's vulnerable pressure hull, and the ballast tank began filling with water. The submarine listed to port a couple of degrees, but this was corrected by intentionally flooding a similar tank on the opposite side.

"The damage didn't cause us any problem," said Commander Axene, who described the damage as "unimportant." But, because of the forthcoming shock tests, it was decided to have the tank inspected and repaired before going on to Key West. A fast check revealed that the nearest drydock that could immediately take the *Thresher* was back at the Electric Boat yard in Groton. Quickly the *Thresher* headed out to sea and made a high-speed, submerged run back to Groton. There the *Thresher* was brought into drydock. Eighteen hours later she was afloat again, the tug's damage to her repaired.

The shock tests would have two purposes: They would determine what physical effects underwater explosions would have on the submarine and what effect they would have on the submarine's noise output. For the latter phase of the tests, careful checks would be made on the *Thresher*'s noise output before, during, and after the shock test.

First the submarine headed for Tongue of the Ocean and a preliminary noise test. Then she steamed to Key West. There a test course was carefully laid out. Slowly the *Thresher* steamed on various headings while a surface ship exploded submerged charges at fixed distances from the submerged submarine. Gradually the intensity of the charges was increased.

The noise inside the submarine was terrifying, and the *Thresher* sustained some damage: Rivets in metal lockers inside the submarine broke loose, cabinet doors flew open, tubes in electronic gear shattered or were jarred loose from their sockets. The tests continued for two weeks. After each series the *Thresher*'s noise output was carefully measured at Key West. Then she went out again to be subjected to more blasting.

During those two weeks the *Thresher* was subjected to a greater intentional pounding than any other submarine in the history of the U.S. Navy. But she stood up "remarkably well," according to Commander Axene. "There was no question that the *Thresher* suffered damage," he said. "But it was all relatively minor. . . . The damage we sustained did not impair the ship's ability to operate, and much of it, such as the damage to vital sonar tubes, we could repair ourselves with our store of spare parts."

July 4 found the *Thresher* back at Tongue of the Ocean being checked for noise output. It was important to know if the two weeks of pounding had caused the *Thresher*'s machinery to produce more noise or if any "creaks and groans" had been created that would produce underwater noise and make her easier for an enemy to find.

With the results of the shock tests adding new laurels to the *Thresher,* Commander Axene pointed his submarine back north for Portsmouth. In mid-July she put to sea again from Portsmouth with some VIPs—Very Important Persons. To the men of the *Thresher* they were the most important ever to come aboard—their families. Now the *Thresher* showed off for the wives, parents, and children of the men who manned her. It was a "happy cruise." For the wives it revealed the black hull that was the "other woman" in their husbands' lives, for the parents it was a look at their son's pride and joy, and for the children . . . well, what could be more exciting than a ride in daddy's atomic submarine?

The submarine's next cruise would bring heartbreak, agony, and despair to most of the dependents who went to sea in the *Thresher* that day.

CHAPTER 3

IN THE YARD

Submariners do not like shipyard overhauls. Whenever possible the Navy will send a sailor's family to his ship's home port. Although the *Thresher* was based at New London, most of her families were still in the Portsmouth area where she had been built. The sailors whose families were not in Portsmouth had to pay their own expenses if they wished to have the families there for the overhaul period. It was not an easy decision. Was it worth the money to bring the family in? Or would it be cheaper to travel to them when he could? Could a home be sublet to help finance the family's moving for the few months? What about school for the kids?

There are other reasons why crews dislike shipyard overhauls. The submarine is the home of the submariner. He spends more time living, eating, working, and sleeping in his submarine than any other single place. He knows the submarine. He knows just when to tilt his head sideways so his skull does not strike a protruding valve. He knows exactly where the light switches are and how to adjust the shower. He has his favorite seat in the mess hall. And he keeps his submarine immaculate. This is often the first observation made by visitors to a submarine, especially members of foreign navies who invariably comment on the cleanliness of U.S. undersea craft.

To the submariner his ship is his home and pride.

Then comes the shipyard.

As the submarine begins her overhaul all personal gear is removed, along with all spare parts and such pilferable items as clocks, binoculars, ship's cameras, navigation instruments, ash trays, and the like. The submarine is stripped of all items that belong to the individual or the government and which are not welded or bolted down.

The officers and leading petty officers meet with yard officials and senior shop men to discuss each and every item of work. Although each work request has been previously submitted and approved by technical bureaus in Washington, by the Atlantic Fleet's Submarine Force commander, and by the yard's planning department, hot arguments sometimes ensue about exactly what work will be done on a particular item of equipment.

The men move into barracks ashore. An office is also set up ashore. All power within the submarine is secured. Electrical power is carried onto the submarine from the dock. Electric cables and air hoses begin snaking their way throughout the submarine, running through hatches and watertight doors, creating a sense of uneasiness in the ever-cautious submariner who never feels secure when he cannot make his ship watertight.

At first only a few yard workmen come aboard. The submarine's overhaul has just begun. Other submarines in later stages of overhaul and construction have priority. But soon more and more "yard birds" come aboard. The workmen do not have any emotional feeling for the submarine. Why should they? To them the submarine is an inert piece of metal, just another job. Linoleum, previously as polished as the kitchen floor at home, is torn up; equipment is gouged out of the submarine and taken into the cluster of nearby shops; wires are left dangling from bulkheads; dirt accumulates; hundreds of pipes are disconnected; deck plates are removed; wooden boards take the place of decks here and there; and noisy blowers are installed to remove fumes.

Piles of rubbish start growing everywhere, springing up hourly as workmen discard stripped wires, metal filings, paper, wood chips, torn rubber linings, and an almost endless list of other debris.

This was the submariner's home. The workmen have turned the submarine into a metal shell seemingly filled with junk and rubbish. The natural antagonism again begins between the ordinary submariners and the ordinary yard workmen.

The submarine's commanding officer is still responsible for the safety of his ship. His crew is still responsible for her cleanliness. Both become almost impossible responsibilities. The yard workmen work an exact eight-hour day. They drop whatever they are doing when the time to quit work arrives. The sailors usually work a 12-to-17-hour day in the yard; even longer if necessary, another source of antagonism.

Workers eat their lunches on the job and throw their trash on the decks or "hide" it behind pipes. Few use trash cans. The heaps of rubbish grow. On occasion, pools of urine are found in "corners" of the submarine.

No official communication can take place between a submariner and a yard workman. If a sailor observes a yard man performing improperly he must take his badge number and report via his own officers to the "ship's superintendent," a naval officer who is the only official liaison between the submarine and the yard. It is difficult to pin down responsibility for a job improperly done. Usually the yard repeats the job, and a second cost is added to the budget of the Submarine Force commander. Sometimes the yard stands behind its work and makes the second repair without further "visible" cost. But in these cases the yard's "overhead" goes up; that is, the cost of every repair job is raised a slight amount.

Yet many close, lifetime relationships are formed between submariners and yard workmen, especially between the leading enlisted men and the senior workmen, masters, quartermen, and foremen.

Said Commander Axene, "Relations between *Thresher* and Portsmouth were always extraordinarily good, at least in my experience." However, he quickly added: "It is true that we felt they should have been more efficient, should have done better work at times, and more quickly, and that they should have done a better job of cleaning up after themselves. I was told by others that relations did deteriorate toward the end of the PSA" [Post Shakedown Availability].

During the *Thresher*'s time in the yard, many openings were cut in her pressure hull to allow removal of machinery and installation of new pipes, wires, and other things that had to pass through the submarine's pressure hull. Despite the uneasy feeling of submariners when they see direct sunlight shining into their engine rooms, Commander Axene was not concerned about the openings cut in the *Thresher*. "They probably had no bearing on the integrity of the ship when the overhaul was finished," he said later. For, after being welded closed again, the pressure hull of the *Thresher* would be carefully X-rayed to insure no flaws in its integrity remained.

When the *Thresher*—termed a submarine only through force of habit while she was in the yard—was some three months into her overhaul, Commander Axene received orders for "duty as Officer-in-Charge, *John C. Calhoun* (SSB(N)-630), from time that vessel is placed in service, special, including period of builder's trials, and as Commanding Officer (Blue Crew) USS *John C. Calhoun* (SSBN(N)-630), when placed in commission."

The *John C. Calhoun* was one of the giant, 425-foot Polaris missile submarines being built at Newport News, Virginia. She would be a first cousin to the *Thresher,* fast and deep-diving. But instead of an elaborate sonar suit backed up with the SUBROC sub-killing missile, the *Calhoun* would have a main battery of 16 Polaris A-3 missiles with a range of some 2,500 nautical miles. Their nuclear warheads would be able to inflict more destructive force than the combined power of all explosives used by the United States in World War II, including the two atom bombs dropped on Japan. The *John C. Calhoun* was a prized command. But Dean Axene didn't want her, not yet anyway.

"I was unhappy with the orders and wanted to stay with the *Thresher,*" he later recalled. "I felt the overhaul was unfinished business, and I wanted to turn the *Thresher* over to my relief as an operating unit."

Commander Axene protested the orders, but without result. Next, Captain Andrews, commander of Submarine Development Group 2 and Axene's immediate superior, protested the orders. But they were still not changed. The Polaris program had the highest national priority and the top submariners were needed to man the missile-firing submarines coming off the building ways. Commander Axene liked the compliment, but not the orders. After Captain Andrews' protest had been turned down, Commander Axene decided not to push the matter any further.

The *Thresher*'s overhaul continued.

In January 1963, Commander Axene's relief on the Navy's most advanced attack submarine reported aboard. He was 36-year-old Lieutenant Commander John Wesley Harvey, an outstanding officer. A Naval Academy graduate, he too had been in the nuclear submarine program almost as long as the Navy had such craft.

The *Thresher's* new skipper liked football (as did his predecessor), and had played for Frankford High School in Philadelphia. Harvey stood first in his high-school class and won a scholarship to the University of Pennsylvania, where he studied for a year before entering the Naval Academy. Harvey was graduated from Annapolis in 1950 and, with the single gold stripe of ensign on his sleeve, he served on an aircraft carrier before reporting to submarine training in June of 1951. His first duty as a submariner was aboard the diesel-electric boat *Sea Robin*. While he served in the World War II-built sub, the revolutionary nuclear-propelled submarine *Nautilus* was being built.

Harvey applied for nuclear power training under Rickover, then a captain. After successfully completing the grueling course in nuclear training, Harvey received orders to the most advanced warship then afloat, the *Nautilus*. In the important billet of reactor control officer he was aboard the *Nautilus* on August 3, 1958, when the submarine became the first ship in history to reach the North Pole.

Harvey first came into the public limelight in the fall of 1958. Television producers were seeking personable young heroes for their quiz shows. (Marine Corps pilot John Glenn was a contestant in his pre-astronaut days. At the time he had just set a jet plane record.) Harvey, then a lieutenant just back from the *Nautilus's* epic polar cruise, was asked to try out for the National Broadcasting Company daytime show "Concentration." On the show he managed to solve the rebus puzzle ahead of his competitor often enough to win an estimated $4,500 worth of prizes consisting of a car, a pair of table lighters, a set of electric trains, a motion picture projector, two tickets to the show "My Fair Lady," an electric can opener, a mink stole, a Swedish-made motorbike, and a mud bath. All of the presents—except possibly the mud bath—were welcomed by Harvey's wife Irene and their two sons, then aged four and seven.

Harvey's star was on the rise: From the *Nautilus* he went to shore duty in the nuclear submarine program as chief engineer for a land-based submarine reactor at Windsor, Connecticut. This was an exact replica of the nuclear reactor that would go into the submarine *Tullibee,* then under construction. In this way, new reactor designs for nuclear ships are fully tested and proved before the ships themselves go to sea; they also serve as training devices for the submarine crewmen. Harvey then helped fit out the *Tullibee,* which was being built at Groton in an attempt to develop a small, specialized hunter-killer submarine that would lie in wait for Soviet undersea craft, either outside of their ports or in narrow waterways as they sought to enter the open oceans.

The *Tullibee* was the first submarine to be fitted with a sonar suit in her bow, with her torpedo tubes moved farther aft. Originally planned to be a 900-ton craft, the *Tullibee* grew to 2,177 tons because of her reactor requirements and other considerations. The *Tullibee* was the only submarine built to this design because the Navy opted instead to build the more versatile *Thresher*-type submarines. When the *Tullibee* was commissioned in late 1960, Harvey was her engineer officer.

His next step was clearly an indication of things to come. In May 1961, Harvey—with the rank of lieutenant commander—became executive officer of the nuclear submarine Seadragon. The Seadragon, built at the Portsmouth Naval Shipyard, was based at Pearl Harbor, Hawaii, which she had reached by sailing through a channel of the fabled Northwest

Passage through the Canadian archipelago, with a side trip to the North Pole. She had already made her mark, but a more historic voyage was still to come.

With Harvey as her executive officer, on July 12, 1962, the *Seadragon* headed north toward the narrow passage between Soviet Siberia and American Alaska. The *Seadragon* passed between the two land masses and dived under the Arctic ice pack. On July 31 she made an under-ice rendezvous with the nuclear submarine *Skate*, which had sailed from an East Coast port. The two submarines met north of the Siberian islands of Severnaya Zemlya, just over 100 nautical miles from the nearest Soviet territory and about 330 nautical miles from the Soviet mainland. It was the first multi-sub operation under the Arctic ice pack. Together the submarines headed for the North Pole and surfaced at the top of the world. After ceremonies at the Pole they submerged together, carried out joint exercises, and then returned to their respective bases.

Being executive officer of a submarine is the final step in training before command. And command at sea is a goal of almost every naval officer. Nearly every facet in the training of a line officer, from his first classes at the Naval Academy to the billet of exec, is designed to prepare him for the position of commanding officer. Indeed, the executive officer of a ship is second in command, and, should the commanding officer be absent or incapacitated, the exec must be qualified to take command of the ship without hesitation. It was no surprise when Harvey was ordered to command a nuclear-propelled submarine—the *Thresher*.

The arriving and departing skippers of the *Thresher* were old shipmates. They had served together briefly in both the *Sea Robin* and *Nautilus*. Together, Commander Axene and Lieutenant Commander Harvey went over the *Thresher* as she was being overhauled at Portsmouth. When a commanding officer is ordered to a ship in the midst of overhaul he has a chance to see what is inside her "skin" and sections of her that are not normally accessible. Now the two skippers went over the *Thresher.* Seeing the submarine in this torn-down condition was of tremendous value to Commander Harvey. It showed him exactly how the *Thresher* was put together.

The end of the *Thresher*'s overhaul, which had stretched to nine months, was in sight when her new skipper took over. There were several reasons for the lengthy wait: The *Thresher* was the first submarine of her design and invariably prototypes have many "bugs." Most of her equipment—especially her huge AN/BQQ-2 sonar suit—was new and needed modifications and alterations.

Equipment overhauled in shops ashore was tested in the shop with a member of the submarine's crew present, returned to the submarine, installed, and tested again. If the submarine's inspector was satisfied, he reported so to the proper submarine department head who then "signed off" the job. A check-off sheet was kept for each of the *Thresher*'s 875 work requests. Each one was meticulously checked off, one-by-one, day-by-day. Unsatisfactory work was marked for redoing. Sometimes marginal work would not be immediately redone if it would postpone sea trials and was not of vital importance. Reportedly, all but five work requests—and those were described as relatively minor—were satisfactorily handled.

After all the large machinery was reinstalled, "hard patches" were placed over the openings in the *Thresher*'s hull and carefully welded into place. Then the welds were X-rayed to assure they were done properly and the hull's circumference along these hard patches was carefully measured to insure that there were no corners or "flatness." The hull had to be precisely circular to distribute evenly over the hull the immense pressures that the submarine would soon experience.

As the *Thresher* neared the end of her yard period, the crew began cleaning the ship as thoroughly as possible every four hours, attempting not only to keep up with the accumulation of excess materials, trash, and other disposables, but also to gain ground and make the submarine a home again. Formica that lined compartment bulkheads was replaced, and damaged floor linoleum was relaid.

Every day the *Thresher* began to look more like a fighting ship again. Additional tests were made on equipment as more systems became operational in the submarine, and then the *Thresher* underwent her "fast cruise." While moored alongside a pier, the submarine was sealed and all equipment that could be was tested. The *Thresher*'s propeller was even tested while wire cables held the submarine securely to the pier.

Still more tests were made. Emergency drills were conducted. A feeling of anticipation or "getting under way fever" pervaded the crew. The normally long working days of the *Thresher*'s crew stretched still further into the nights. At last, food, navigating instruments, ash trays, some personal belongings, and mattresses, sheets, and blankets were brought aboard.

The end was in sight.

CHAPTER 4

THE LAST CRUISE

At 3:45 on the morning of April 9, 1963 the piers of the Portsmouth Naval Shipyard were cold and damp. The darkness was broken here and there by the glare of streetlights and floodlights. Resting quietly in the waters of the Piscataqua River, the nuclear submarine *Thresher* was securely moored to Pier 11 at the shipyard. Inside most of the submarine's compartments it was bright as day. Power lines connected with the shipyard provided electricity for lights, radios, cooking, and a dozen other household duties. The submarine's nuclear power plant was still.

Fifteen minutes before the hour of four, Lieutenant Commander John S. Lyman, the *Thresher*'s engineer officer, began the four-hour countdown required for starting up the submarine's atomic power plant. Two hours later he requested permission to pull the first control rods which would start the reactor "cooking." These rods were are made of special metals that absorb neutrons from the uranium 235 "fuel" in the reactor. As the rods were removed, fewer neutrons are absorbed until there are enough "free" neutrons to split other atoms.

The atom-splitting produces still more neutrons that make possible a sustained nuclear reaction.

Lieutenant Commander Harvey, the *Thresher*'s commanding officer, gave permission to pull the rods.

A nuclear "fire" was silently lit.

At 6:15 the engineer officer reported to Harvey that the reactor had gone "critical," meaning it had reached the point of self-sustained nuclear fission. An hour later, the submarine's turbo-electric generator was producing electricity to feed the innumerable pieces of equipment that did everything from cook eggs to compute torpedo firing angles. At 7:30, the engine room notified Harvey that the full power of the submarine's remarkable propulsion system was ready to respond to orders.

One by one the lines holding the *Thresher* to Pier 11 were cast off. Soon there was nothing connecting the 129 men aboard the submarine with the shore. Normally only a 104-man crew plus perhaps a few men for training would be aboard. But, because the *Thresher* was going out on post-overhaul trials, there were also shipyard personnel and representatives of the Atlantic Fleet Submarine Force, the Naval Ordnance Laboratory, and civilian firms with special equipment in the submarine. In all, there were 12 officers and 96 men assigned to the submarine; a Submarine Force staff officer; three officers and 13 civilian employees from the Portsmouth yard; a specialist from the Naval Ordnance Laboratory in White Oak, Maryland; and three civilian factory representatives.

Four men who would normally have gone out in the *Thresher* that morning stayed ashore: Lieutenant Raymond J. McCoole, 33, was not aboard the *Thresher* on her final voyage because his wife had suffered a minor accident at home. The morning before—20 hours before the *Thresher* was to go to sea—McCoole's wife Barbara called him at the shipyard and said: "I feel terrible about calling you, but something dreadful has happened." She explained that while opening a bottle of rubbing alcohol some had spurted into her eyes.

McCoole quickly found Lieutenant Commander Pat Garner, exec of the *Thresher*, and explained what had happened. Then McCoole rushed back to his home, eight miles from the shipyard. His wife had flushed her eyes with water, but they still burned and she could not see clearly. He took her to a nearby hospital where she was given emergency treatment, and her eyes were bandaged.

The McCooles had five children, their ages then ranging from six months to nine years. With Barbara having to keep her eyes bandaged for several days, McCoole could not leave her alone. He phoned the yard and explained what had happened. Garner told him to stay put. McCoole said he wanted to make the cruise and would try to find a nurse to stay with the family. Reportedly Garner replied: "I'm ordering you to stay with Barbara. . . . Besides, we can use the room for one of the civilian technicians. Don't worry, Ray, there'll be plenty more trips for you."

Three enlisted men assigned to the *Thresher* were also ashore when she sailed. Garron S. Weitzel, 27, an interior communications electrician second class, had been attending navigation school at Dam Neck, Virginia, since January. He was scheduled to return to the *Thresher* in June. Frank DeStefano, a 29-year-old chief machinist's mate, had been sent to Washington for an interview with Vice Admiral Rickover in preparation for further assignment in the Navy's nuclear power program. He was also in line for a commission. Raymond Mattson, 34, a torpedoman's mate first class, had been ordered ashore for treatment of a nervous condition.

The large black submarine that was the *Thresher* eased away from the pier slowly. She steamed south, around New Castle Island, out of sight of the sprawling shipyard, and into the open sea off Odiorenes Point. As she met the running sea, she wallowed. The *Thresher*—shaped somewhat like a giant fish—was designed for high submerged speeds. On the surface her hull design made her cantankerous and unsteady.

As the *Thresher* pulled away from the New England coast, she began a series of surface trials that included tests of her communication and navigation equipment. East of Boston, at 9:49 a.m. the *Thresher* rendezvoused with the submarine rescue ship *Skylark*. The *Skylark* would escort the *Thresher* on her diving tests as was the custom in the Navy. The *Skylark* would provide a communications link to shore and, if the *Thresher* ran into trouble, try to assist her.

Skippered by Lieutenant Commander Stanley W. Hecker, the 205-foot *Skylark* was designed to help men escape from sunken submarines. Rescue ships have six anchors and several buoys so they can moor directly over a sunken submarine. On board are divers and elaborate equipment to bring them down to investigate a stricken submarine and, if possible, to attach hoses to pump in air for breathing or to "blow" the submarine to the surface. On the deck of every rescue ship is a submarine rescue chamber. This device, developed in the late 1920s, is a two-chamber diving bell that can be sent down to a stricken submarine, attached to a hatch, take on survivors, and carry them to the surface. In the first—and so far only—use of the chamber, 33 men were brought up from the sunken U.S. submarine *Squalus* in 1939. (Another 26 men lost their lives when flooding compartments in the submarine were closed off to save the rest of the crew.)

The *Squalus* sank in 240 feet of water. The rescue chamber can aid submarines in water as deep as 850 feet. Thus, if anything was to happen to the *Thresher* while over the continental shelf—the submerged coastal area where the water is less than 600 feet deep—the *Skylark* might be able to save anyone trapped in the stricken submarine. But if the submarine went down in deeper waters, and crewmen were alive, there was no means of rescuing them.

The *Skylark* had orders to meet the *Thresher* and escort the submarine on her diving tests. No agenda of the *Thresher's* tests had been given to the *Skylark*. Later the rescue ship's commanding officer related, "I had no information as to the capabilities of the *Thresher* such as her depth, speed, and range. In fact, the UQC [Navy jargon for underwater telephone] was the only equipment on the *Skylark* of known capability with submarines."

With the *Skylark* standing nearby, the *Thresher* made a shallow dive, checking for leaks and testing various equipment. After this initial shallow test dive, the *Thresher* came to the surface. Throughout this shallow test dive conversations were carried on between the *Thresher* and *Skylark* with the UQC, which is actually like an underwater "acoustic" radio. The quality of communication between a surface ship and a submarine varies as sea conditions and distance between the ships change. As water temperature and density change between the two ships, the sound waves are often deflected and distorted, and what is received by the surface ship is sometimes garbled.

As the *Thresher* again wallowed on the surface, Harvey released the *Skylark* and directed the rescue ship to rendezvous again with the submarine the next morning for deep-dive tests some 200 nautical miles east of Cape Cod. The deep-dive tests were to be conducted beyond the continental shelf where the water drops off rapidly to more than 8,000 feet. While the *Thresher*'s diving capability did not approach that depth, she did need more than the 600 feet of depth available over the continental shelf.

About 3 p.m. on the afternoon of April 9 the *Thresher* again slipped beneath the waves and headed for the rendezvous point. En route various tests were conducted, including a full-power run with the submarines making about 30 knots. That night, as the *Thresher* sped toward deeper water, she transmitted a routine radio check to Atlantic Fleet Submarine Force Headquarters at Norfolk, Virginia.

At 6:35 on the fateful morning of April 10, the *Thresher* came up to periscope depth some ten nautical miles from the *Skylark*. It was the last time John Harvey saw the light of day. At 7:47 a.m. the *Thresher* notified the *Skylark* by underwater telephone that she was preparing to dive to her test depth. Here the term "test" is somewhat misleading. The test depth of a nuclear submarine is the maximum depth at which she is designed to operate and fight. Before the *Thresher* entered the yard for her nine-month overhaul she had been to her test depth some 40 times. That depth—long considered highly classified—was 1,300 feet. (At the time the Navy would officially say that U.S. nuclear submarines could dive "deeper than 400 feet.")

Submarine skippers have strict orders not to go below the craft's test depth except in the most dire emergency. Below test depth the fittings and pipes on the submarine begin to give way. Deeper, the tremendous pressure would begin to "pull" the submarine's hardened steel like taffy. Through the ruptured pipes, fittings, and hull, tons of water would shoot in, flooding the submarine in seconds or driving her to depths where the intense pressure would smash her in.

But Lieutenant Commander Harvey had no intention of taking his submarine below her test depth. During her test-depth dive the *Thresher* would level off at certain depths to check for leaks and to test equipment. She was to notify the *Skylark* of changes of course, depth, speed, and, in any event, make a telephone check every 15 minutes. The telephone messages would be recorded in the written logs aboard both ships.

Thirteen minutes before the hour of 8 o'clock the *Thresher* reported to the *Skylark* by underwater telephone that she was beginning her test-depth dive. Five minutes later, the *Thresher* reported being at 400 feet and checking for leaks.

Two minutes later—at 7:54—the *Thresher* told the *Skylark* that future references to depth would be made in terms of test depth to prevent discussions from being intercepted by any craft in the area, especially the numerous Soviet trawlers that cruise off the American coast. Thus, references to test depth were given without using actual figures.

At 8:09 a.m. the *Thresher* reported she was at one-half her test depth; at 8:35, "minus 300 feet." Eighteen minutes later, a message said the submarine was proceeding to test depth.

At 9:02, the *Thresher* asked for a repetition of a course reading, according to Lieutenant (junior grade) James D. Watson, the *Skylark's* navigator, who was talking with the submarine. He later said the *Skylark* had good communication with the *Thresher* at the time. Ten minutes later the two vessels made a routine check.

Then, "about a minute later," according to Lieutenant Watson, the *Thresher* reported: "Have positive up angle. . . . Attempting to blow up." Others aboard the *Skylark* who heard the message remembered it differently. Lieutenant Commander Hecker recalled the voice over the underwater telephone as having said: "Experiencing minor problem. . . . Have positive angle. . . . Attempting to blow." Roy S. Mowen Jr., a boatswain's mate third class, recalled the *Thresher's* last message as: "Experiencing minor difficulty. . . . Have positive up angle. . . . Attempting to blow. . . . Will keep you informed."

The *Skylark's* written log—the official record—recorded that at 9:12 a "satisfactory" underwater telephone check was made. Subsequently, it showed the submarine reported: "Have position up angle. . . . Attempting to blow up." Contrary to Navy procedure, the exact time of this message was not recorded.

Thus, it is known only that just after 9:12 the *Thresher* indicated she was having some kind of difficulty. Then the men aboard the *Skylark* listening to the UQC heard the sounds of air under high pressure.

At 9:14 the *Skylark* told the *Thresher* she had no contact. The submarine was asked to give her course and bearing to the *Skylark*. There was no reply. Hecker, skipper of the *Skylark,* told the man at the microphone to ask: "Are you in control?" When there was no reply, Hecker took the microphone himself and repeated the question three times.

But nothing was heard from the submarine until 9:17 when a garbled message was heard. To Hecker the message was unintelligible. But Watson believed that last garbled message from the *Thresher* ended with the distinct words "test depth." Seconds later, Watson heard a sound he remembered from his World War II days—"the sound of a ship breaking up . . . like a compartment collapsing."

Taking careful check of his position at the time of the last communication with the *Thresher,* Hecker patrolled the area, listening attentively for some reply to his continued calls to the submarine. At 10:58, the *Skylark* began dropping small signal grenades into the water. This is a pre-arranged signal with submarines to surface in case communications are lost. At almost the same time, Hecker ordered a radio message sent to New London, where the *Thresher* was assigned to Submarine Development Group 2 which in turn was part of Submarine Flotilla 2.

Far from being an alarm, the message tended merely to indicate a communications failure: UNABLE TO COMMUNICATE WITH THRESHER SINCE 0917. HAVE BEEN CALLING BY UQC VOICE AND CW QRB CW [dot-dash code] EVERY MINUTE EXPLOSIVE SIGNALS EVERY 10 MINS WITH NO SUCCESS. LAST TRANSMISSION RECD [received] WAS GARBLED. INDICATED THRESHER WAS APPROACHING TEST DEPTH. MY PRESENT POSITION 41–43N 64–57W CONDUCTING EXPANDING SEARCH.

The message was sent with an "operational immediate" priority. This meant it was to be sent and delivered as fast as possible. The two higher priorities in naval communications are reserved for vital emergencies, such as contact with enemy forces. The *Thresher* was not in emergency, not yet at least. The wording of the *Skylark*'s message would put the Navy's search procedure in action.

But sending the "operational immediate" signal took time. The *Skylark* is an auxiliary ship, not a warship with elaborate radio equipment that can flash a message around the world in seconds. Her communications link to the shore was a transmitter broadcasting dot-dash signals. As Robert L. Cartwright, radioman first class, tapped out the fateful message, atmospheric conditions made transmission difficult. Several times the radio operator at New London had to interrupt the *Skylark*'s transmission with requests to repeat portions of the message.

It took one hour and 58 minutes to send the brief message from the *Skylark* to New London. Captain J. Sneed Schmidt, commander of Submarine Flotilla 2, received the *Skylark*'s message at 1:02 p.m. as he returned from lunch. "I had two officers from *Norfolk* as my guests," he recalled later. "The chief handed me the paper and said, 'Here's a message you've got to see right away.' I looked at it, read it aloud, and said, 'Now gentlemen, you can see the importance of this. You'll excuse me while I get going.' "

Captain Schmidt later recalled that he had no feeling of disaster as he read the radio message. "It's happened many times before where ships have lost communication. I get messages like this every week on the average."

But there was no question that action must be taken "just in case." The direct-line "hot phone" from New London to Atlantic Fleet Headquarters at Norfolk quickly carried the text of the *Skylark*'s message to the top operating commanders on the East Coast. Within the hour, Vice Admiral Elton W. Grenfell, commander of all submarines in the Atlantic, and Captain Schmidt were discussing the *Skylark* message by phone. "We agreed that this doesn't look good," Schmidt later said.

Another Norfolk-based flag officer, Vice Admiral Wallace Beakley, was told of the *Skylark* message at 1:32 p.m. Five minutes later, in his capacity as Deputy Commander-in-Chief of the Atlantic Fleet, he ordered the nuclear submarine *Seawolf*, the diesel-electric submarine *Sea Owl*, the rescue ship *Sunbird*, and an aircraft to the scene of the *Thresher*'s last reported position. Shortly afterwards the salvage ship *Recovery* and additional aircraft were ordered into the search.

Back at New London, Captain Frank A. Andrews, the commander of Submarine Development Group 2, climbed into a helicopter and was flown out to the large destroyer *Norfolk* that was cruising off Cape Cod. After taking him aboard, the sleek *Norfolk* picked up speed and headed to the search area while Captain Andrews made preparations for taking charge of the various ships, submarines, and aircraft racing eastward to join the hunt for the *Thresher*.

The Navy's No. 1 officer, Chief of Naval Operations George W. Anderson, was told of the *Thresher* situation about 3:40 p.m. Admiral Anderson had been attending a meeting of the Joint Chiefs of Staff in the Pentagon, which concluded at 3:35. While he was walking back to his office from the meeting, Atlantic Fleet Headquarters phoned his office on a "hot line" circuit. Admiral Claude V. Ricketts, the Vice Chief of Naval Operations, took the call and was told that communications between the *Skylark* and *Thresher* had been lost and that the submarine might be in trouble. Ricketts immediately sent his senior aide to find Admiral Anderson and inform him of the message.

The aide, Captain H.B. Sweitzer, encountered Admiral Anderson in the corridor outside of the E-ring office of Secretary of the Navy Fred Korth. Admiral Anderson stepped into Korth's office and repeated the message he had just received. After a brief conversation, Korth called the White House to speak to Captain Tazewell T. Shepard, the President's naval aide. Fifteen minutes later Captain Shepard was in Mr. Kennedy's office.

John F. Kennedy—the first American president to have worn the uniform of a naval officer—asked first how many men were involved. Shepard did not have the exact number involved, but told the Commander-in-Chief that the normal complement of such a submarine was about 90 men. "The President asked me to keep him informed of the search efforts," Captain Shepard was to recall later. "He was very distressed at the possibility that the submarine may have been lost."

Far to the north, the Canadian Navy was asked to stand by to assist in whatever operations might be necessary. The *Thresher*'s last reported position was only about 100 nautical miles off the tip of Nova Scotia. Canadian Navy Headquarters at Halifax on the Nova Scotia peninsula quickly alerted one of the submarines based there to stand by to get under way. As the submarine's skipper ordered his crew rounded up, a rumor began to spread that a U.S. submarine was in trouble.

A newsman at television station CJCH heard the rumor and the station interrupted its program with the bulletin: "U.S. submarine reported in danger of sinking or in trouble on the high seas."

The secret was out.

CHAPTER 5

INSIDE THE *THRESHER*

Submarine trials are invariably hectic. The boat has not been to sea for months; nine months in the case of the *Thresher*. Many crewmen, although experienced sailors and submariners, are new to the *Thresher*. They have trained for long hours with training devices, on board other submarines, and by study and discussion. Still, this is different.

Much new equipment has been installed in the *Thresher* which, though tested at the factory, in the shipyard, and in the submarine while alongside a dock, has not operated in its natural environment. Machinery, fittings, pipes, and innumerable other items have been extensively tested aboard the moored submarine. However, they have not been tested on board a moving, vibrating submarine, slamming through rough seas.

The crewmen have been working long hours in the final preparation for sea trials. For the next two or three days they will have little sleep, plenty of coffee, and much hard work. But there is a spirit of revivification. The "old girl" has been tied up so long that many have forgotten what a beauty the submarine really is. She handles like a dream once she is in her own element, running fast and deep.

The men of the *Thresher* have been anxious to get back to sea, to leave the yard and its clock-watching civilian workers, and get back to business. The older chief petty officers know that it will take a couple of months back in operation to get all the wrinkles out, shed all vestiges of the yard, and work the crew into the well-organized, closely-knit professional team that it was nine months ago.

As the *Thresher* pulls away from the pier and swings out into the channel, everyone is busy. The navigator is taking bearings on fixed objects on the shore. Only a few charts are on board—enough to get to the sea trial operating area; a few pencils are on the chart table.

"Chief, you did bring the almanac, didn't you?"

"Yes, sir."

Elsewhere in the control room the helmsman is sitting in the right-hand "pilot" seat; the standby helmsman and planesman is sitting in the left hand seat—just the reverse of the pilot and copilot positions of a large aircraft. Both men are watching dials and pointers on the control panel. While still on the surface there are only a few dials to watch. The depth and vertical angle of the submarine need not be controlled while on the surface.

Behind the "pilots" stands the officer of the watch who is in charge of the control room. On the port side sits the chief of the watch, a senior enlisted man who is in charge of the diving panel or ballast control board. From this station the submarine's main ballast tanks can be filled to make her "heavier"; internal ballast can be shifted; and the main ballast tanks can be blown empty with compressed air.

Electricians, communications personnel, and others combine to make the control room a beehive of activity with perhaps a dozen men at their stations. High above the control room the commanding officer—always "captain" to his crew regardless of his rank—stands on the small bridge atop the sail or fairwater structure as the boat follows the channel to sea.

From below: "God, I'll be happy to get my gear on board once and for all. How I hate yard overhauls."

The *Thresher* passes the sea buoy. "Man, it's good to be at sea again."

The air freshens; there are fewer birds following; the first ocean swell surrounds the boat; the *Thresher* pitches a little more; a gentle roll is now noticeable.

"Secure the maneuvering watch; set the regular sea detail. Section two has the watch."

"Hey, Joe, you see the watch list?"

"Mann, lay up to the control room."

Those not on watch gather for a moment in the crew's mess. A flush of excitement is on everyone. Coffee—the Navy uses almost as much as it does fuel oil—pours into china coffee mugs. Some mugs have the owner's rating insignia painted on them. Other the *Thresher's* emblem. "This sure beats that damn stuff they call coffee ashore," someone invariably says.

Throughout the submarine the real work of the cruise begins. It looks as if everyone has a sheaf of papers. Check-off lists for making hundreds of tests throughout the submarine are attached to clipboards. Pencils jot check-marks and digits as the holders read a dial, check a switch, test a circuit.

"Where in the hell are the three-amp fuses?"

"Go see if you can talk the stewards out of some toilet paper; the captain of the head forgot to bring any along."

"Hell, what are you squawking about? You won't have time to go to the head."

"Chief, pass the word 'rig for dive'." All hull openings are prepared for quick closing when the order to dive is given.

"Chief, I just inspected the shaft seals. They look real good." The *Thresher's* single propeller shaft pieces the stern of the craft. The seals prevent water from leaking in.

The diving officer is making last-minute computations to insure a reasonable trim on diving. This means that the submarine will submerge with a proper angle and not too steeply. He has already calculated all of the major "inputs"—new equipment, new lead ballast, comparison of difference of the stores on board during the last dive nine months ago and what is estimated now, the spare parts in the storeroom, and all the other big items. The diving officer writes; he checks his slide rule.

"Chief, how many people did we have aboard when we finally got under way?"

"One hundred and twenty-nine, I think. Just a minute, I'll double check with the yeoman, sir."

"Don't bother, that's close enough for government work. Let's see, 129 times an average 150 pounds. . . ."

The initial excitement of again getting under way wears off.

In the maneuvering room the reactor operator stands firmly with his feet apart, hands on hips, and completely alert. His eyes dart up and down and across the many dials which tell him at what temperatures and pressures his machinery is operating. He reaches up to make a minute adjustment in the position of a hand wheel. He has an inner feeling of pride in his machinery-crammed domain which is functioning so well. A smile comes to his face as he looks it over.

The submarine's large geared turbines whine in the machinery spaces, turning the propeller shaft through a series of gears. Hydraulic pumps provide silent power to the ship's rudder that steers the submarine.

Pumps circulate sea water through a maze of pipes to cool a variety of machinery and remove the heat from inside the submarine. Generators powered by the turbine produce the electricity that lights the submarine, makes coffee, works instruments, and provides energy for numerous other devices. The massive air conditioning plant in the submarine produces cold air that blowers circulate throughout the craft. Everywhere in the submarine gauges, dials, and thermometers are watched for warning that one of these systems may not be functioning properly.

The torpedo room is empty of weapons, since submarines do not ordinarily fire weapons on sea trials. However, the torpedomen are busy checking their equipment and making ready for later weapon tests.

What will the *Thresher* do during her three days at sea? Generally all equipment will be tested in a submerged environment and, as a final test of watertight integrity, the submarine will dive to her test depth.

While the *Thresher* was in the yard, work was done on practically every piece of the submarine's equipment. Some work was minor, some major, but, except for short tests, the equipment has been idle for a long time. Idleness is the worst possible state for machinery that is designed to run continuously. Problems continually come up as a submarine on trials heads out to sea. Most are minor. But all have to be traced down and repaired.

The *Thresher*'s first dive would be a shallow one. Regulations state that the initial dive after major hull work will be conducted in water less than 240 feet deep—"just in case." The *Thresher*'s first dive would be to 180 feet. Initially she would level off at about 60 feet so that her extended radar mast would be exposed for contact with the *Skylark*. (Diving depth is measured from the keel, or bottom, of the submarine.)

Then, as she headed out into deeper water during the shallow dive, she would go deeper, but remain well above her test depth. The diving officer has completed his calculations and gives the desired trim tank readings to the chief of the watch. In doing so he subtracts 25,000 pounds from his calculated figure. Better to be lighter than heavier.

The chief then adjusts the water in the submarine's trim tanks.

"Captain, the ship has been compensated and checked. Rigged for dive in all respects. We are approximately one hour from diving point."

"Very well. Pump 25,000 pounds from the auxiliary tanks to the sea."

"Aye aye, sir."

Thus another 25,000 pounds of water are pumped from the submarine's tanks to provide still more buoyancy. Everyone has his own safety factor.

The checks that can be made before submerging continue: Small adjustments are made; minor repairs done; safety circuits are tested; indicators are checked; valve wheels are cleared for quick opening or closing; and the submarine is inspected for signs of leaks.

The *Skylark* comes into sight—a small gray ship with large, bright-orange buoys lashed to her superstructure. The ships close and message are exchanged.

"All personnel take stations for initial dive" is heard throughout the *Thresher.*

This first one will be an extra-careful dive. It will be done by the numbers. Everyone takes it careful and easy.

"Pass the word to secure topside."

The several men on the bridge hurriedly climb down the ladder into the submarine proper, and the hatch leading to the sail secured.

"All secured, sir."

"Pressure in the boat."

A slight air pressure is built up inside the submarine. If the pressure hull can hold this small pressure there can be no major leaks. A minute passes. The pressure holds. The submarine speeds up.

"Sound the diving alarm."

AOOGAH! AOOGAH! The almost indescribable wail of the diving alarm fills the submarine. It abates to be replaced by the sound of air escaping from the ballast tanks as the main vents are opened. As air rushes out through these valves, water takes its place, filling the ballast tanks. Filling the ballast tanks will make the submarine "neutrally buoyant"—not heavy. Rather, she will dive by being propelled forward with her diving planes—at the stern and then on the sail—driving her under water.

The submarine starts to go down bow first. The decks tilt, and 129 men brace themselves a little.

"Make your depth sixty feet."

The boat is slow to dive. Fine—that is normal. She has to be "driven" under. The needle on the depth gauge shows the increase in depth: 40 feet . . . 45 feet . . . 50 feet. . . .

"Flood auxiliary tanks from the sea." Flooding these small tanks will help give the submarine a proper buoyancy or angle of dive.

"Sixty feet, sir."

"Still flooding auxiliary tanks."

"All personnel check their compartments. Report to control." In each compartment are men with earphones and microphones giving them instantaneous communication with the control room. These are sound-powered phones so that an electrical failure will not impair internal communications.

"All ahead one-third."

"Secure flooding auxiliary tanks."

"Captain, all compartments report conditions normal. No leaks."

"Very well. Make your depth 100 feet. Pass the word the ship is going to 100 feet. Check compartments and report to control."

And on the sea trials go. Bit by bit, checking everything. The *Thresher* is a fighting lady. Make sure she is tight . . . tight enough to go down to her test depth and, if necessary, stay there and fight.

A small leak shows up in a sea gauge line. A normal occurrence.

"Secure No. 1 gauge. We'll use No. 2."

The sea valve is shut. The leak stops. A note is made on a clipboard.

"Tell the *Skylark* everything is going fine. We are still heading 120 degrees true."

"Aye aye, sir."

The crewmen now feel as if they have been at sea for a week. "Back in the Saddle Again" hums one sailor as he goes about his work, doing the job he has been training to do for months or perhaps years. Nuclear submarines are complicated craft and to operate them takes extensive training.

"Bracey, how about a cup of coffee? Captain, you want a cup of coffee, sir?"

"Captain, the ship has been checked at 150 feet. No leaks; just few items on the list. Everything looks real good."

As the *Thresher* cruises in the depths, her crew performs a number of special tests, each designed to evaluate another component or function of the submarine. These vary from checking out the toilet-flushing system to running the nuclear reactor at full power. There are more than a thousand of these under-way tests that will check out this magnificent machine for conducting modern warfare, and make certain that every intentional cause produces the intended effect, reliably, quickly, and accurately. Each test is documented for future reference. More checks, figures, and digits are jotted down on the clipboards.

Some tests may fail. The submarine personnel, together with the shipyard experts, note any deviations from the intended effect and attempt to diagnose the problem. These men—Navy and civilian alike—are the experts in the business. The problem might be easily solved, a repair made, and the test repeated. Or, the equipment might need a part not available from the submarine's partially filled spare part bins. A new work request may be made on the spot in preparation for the return to the yard.

Some tests require only a few seconds; others many minutes.

If the failure of a test is serious enough, the sea trials may be stopped. The submarine might even return to port.

There are no major test failures.

The word is passed: "All personnel take stations for test number. . . ."

And on it goes.

After a while the engineer officer stops by the wardroom. "How does it look from your end, John?"

"Just fine," he replies as he nods to a steward, wearing a white jacket, offering him a cup of coffee. He sags into a chair and confers with the captain and others in the wardroom. The tests seem to be going well. All is under control. If the tests continue at the present rate, there should be no reason why the *Thresher* cannot make her deep dive the next morning as scheduled.

Returning to the surface, the *Thresher* dismisses the *Skylark* with orders to rendezvous with her the next morning in the area where the deep dive will be made.

That night the *Thresher* continues east, running submerged in the cold Atlantic waters that are thought to be friendly to her.

CHAPTER 6

THE EARLY SEARCH

On the surface the *Skylark* criss-crossed the area, continuing to call the *Thresher* with her underwater telephone. As the afternoon of April 10 wore on, aircraft and then ships appeared from the west. The aircraft—especially equipped to hunt for Soviet submarines—now used their electronic and magnetic search devices in an effort to find the missing *Thresher.* The ships and submarines combed the area, probing the depths with their sonar.

As the last light of day began to fade, a lookout aboard the salvage ship *Recovery* spotted a calm patch of water in the choppy seas that were beginning to run some four to six feet high. Closer inspection of the calm area showed the water to be covered with oil. Soon the *Skylark* and the *Recovery,* true to her name, began picking up bits of cork and heavy yellow plastic. Both materials are very common to equipment aboard nuclear-powered submarines like the *Thresher.* Although the *Thresher* used uranium for fuel, she carried several thousand gallons of oil for lubrication and for her auxiliary diesel engine.

Floating oil, the age-old indication of a submarine in trouble, and the more positive indication of the cork and plastic debris, tended to confirm the worse fears of those searching for the *Thresher*. The debris shattered what hope there had been that the *Thresher* was somewhere on the dark surface, unheard from because of a communications failure.

And now the Navy began the distressing job of informing relatives of the 129 men aboard the *Thresher* that the submarine was missing and presumed lost. Orders went out that, where possible, Navy men were to personally visit the homes of *Thresher* crewmen to break the tragic news. First, Vice Admiral Grenfell, the Atlantic Fleet's Submarine Force commander, personally phoned Mrs. Harvey to tell her that the *Thresher* was overdue and everything humanly possible was being done to find the submarine, her husband, and his crew.

Notification of the next of kin of those aboard the *Thresher* began about seven on the evening of April 10, with a public announcement set for 8 o'clock that night. On schedule, the Department of Defense released a one-page statement in the name of Admiral Anderson. It said that "the next of kin of the crew of the nuclear submarine USS *Thresher* (SSN-593) are being notified that the ship is overdue and presumed missing."

"Overdue and presumed missing" was the same wording used to announce the loss of United States submarines in World War II. Nuclear submarines were new, and nuclear submarine disasters still newer, so new that there was only the traditional verbiage to fall back on when announcing the worst submarine disaster in history.

There was no use of the terms "sunk" or "lost" in the release, and optimists might even have pointed with hope to this paragraph: "While there is a possibility that the nuclear submarine has not reported her position due to a communication failure, a search was immediately commenced by the

Navy in accordance with emergency proceedings for such situations."

On the fourth floor of the Pentagon building—where Navy leaders work—the lights burned bright into the night. There were few optimists among the gaunt-faced officers and men.

Driving north on the expressway between Boston and Portsmouth the night of April 10, Commander Axene and his wife Sally were returning home after seeing the show "Mary, Mary" in Boston. "We heard a bulletin on the car radio that a submarine was down off the Rhode Island coast," Axene later related. "But we didn't tie it to the *Thresher*; we thought it was somebody operating out of New London."

On the way home, they stopped for dinner, and Commander Axene tried to phone his children at their home in Kittery, Maine, across the Piscataqua River from the Portsmouth Naval Shipyard.

"I called about a half dozen times and kept getting a busy signal," Commander Axene related. "Finally I got through. My son Eric told me the *Thresher* was missing and everyone was trying to get me." The Axenes drove into Portsmouth, Commander Axene going to the shipyard where he had taken command of the *Thresher* some two years earlier. Mrs. Axene went to the home of Mrs. John Lyman, wife of the *Thresher*'s engineer officer and a close friend.

An hour and a half after the Department of Defense news release, Admiral Anderson faced television cameras and reporters. His opening words seemed to be an epitaph to the *Thresher*: "To those of us who have been brought up in the traditions of the sea, one of the saddest occasions is when we lose a ship."

He told of the reported oil slick in the vicinity of the *Thresher*'s last dive and stated that if the submarine sank in 8,400 feet of water "rescue would be absolutely out of the question." He also announced that Vice Admiral Bernard L. Austin would head a formal inquiry into the *Thresher* loss.

The names of those aboard the *Thresher* were still not released, so Navy callers could reach the next of kin before the press did. Some of the families were not at home. Lieutenant McCoole, who had planned to be aboard the *Thresher* that day, was home. McCoole's phone rang. It was Commander Howard N. Larcombe, skipper of the diesel-electric submarine *Dogfish* and the senior submarine commanding officer at Portsmouth.

"How did it go, skipper?" asked McCoole, believing the call was to tell him the *Thresher* was coming in.

"I don't know," replied Larcombe mysteriously. "We haven't heard from her yet. She's overdue."

McCoole had not heard the bulletins about the *Thresher* that were interrupting radio and television programs. He asked Larcombe if he should come down to the yard.

"Well, I'm not going to tell you not to come," said Larcombe.

The tone of Larcombe's voice, the carefully worded replies, told McCoole something was up. Minutes later he was heading for the shipyard.

Someone else making numerous telephone calls the night of April 10 was Vice Admiral Rickover. One was to the Navy's Office of Information, where he advised the naval officers on duty that he was available for any help that they may need from him. He also called Vice Admiral Ralph K. James, Chief of the Bureau of Ships.

"He called to remind me on that occasion," said James, "that he was not the submarine builder, he was simply the nuclear-plant producer." James said that it was the only time in his four-year tenure as chief of the bureau that Rickover was untruthful. James continued: "Rickover went to great extremes to disassociate any likelihood of failure of the nuclear plant from the *Thresher* incident. I considered this thoroughly dishonest."

In the North Atlantic some 220 nautical miles east of Cape Cod it was growing colder, and the seas were running higher and higher. Under the direction of Captain Frank Andrews aboard the large destroyer *Norfolk*, ships and submarines continued to probe the depths with their sonar in an effort to locate the *Thresher*. Sonarmen and radio operators listened for some message from the submarine, still hoping against hope that she was safe somewhere on the surface with her radios out because of an electrical failure.

On the surface were the frigate *Norfolk*, the destroyers *Wallace L. Lind* and *Yarnell*, and the *Skylark* and *Recovery*. Below the surface—but far above the depth to which the *Thresher* could go—the submarines *Seawolf* and *Sea Owl* also searched with their underwater detection gear.

Sonar operators in the *Seawolf* listened carefully as the submarine's sonar searched out—listening for some underwater signal from the *Thresher* or the return from their own sonar beams indicating that they had found the missing submarine. Suddenly, the operators leaned forward, as if they were trying to get closer to a sound that the *Seawolf*'s electronic ears were picking up. They were undoubtedly sonar signals. But hopes that they emanated from the *Thresher* were short-lived.

The *Seawolf*'s reports were radioed to the search commander and ashore. The Navy's submarine specialists quickly determined the sounds were not from the *Thresher*, but probably originated from other ships in the search force and were reflected back to the *Seawolf*, or were water noises.

From Washington came the official statement that "there is absolutely no possibility that the underwater sounds reported in the area where the search for the USS *Thresher* is being conducted could have emanated from the missing submarine." To hopes that the submarine was resting on the bottom of the sea and men trapped in a watertight compartment were sending out the sounds heard by the *Seawolf*, the Navy replied that "no single compartment aboard the *Thresher* could possibly stand this pressure."

About 9:30 on the morning of April 11, Rear Admiral Lawson P. Ramage, deputy commander of submarines in the Atlantic, arrived on the search scene in the destroyer *Blandy*. Admiral Ramage, who as a World War II submarine commander had been awarded the Medal of Honor, the nation's highest decoration, took charge of the search force. On the way were the destroyers *Samuel B. Roberts, Warrington,* and *The Sullivans,* the submarine rescue ship *Sunbird,* the oceanographic research ship *Atlantis II,* and the fleet oiler *Waccamaw,* the last to provide fuel for the other ships while they remained at sea.

When Admiral Ramage arrived at the search scene, he conferred with the *Skylark*'s skipper, Lieutenant Commander Hecker. He summarized the situation for the senior officer, but, according to Ramage, did not mention the *Thresher*'s message of about 9:13 in which the submarine reported she was "experiencing minor problem." Nor did Hecker speak of the *Skylark*'s navigator hearing noises that sounded like a ship breaking up.

Also on the morning of the 11th, Secretary of the Navy Korth and Admiral Grenfell flew up to New London and then Portsmouth. They personally wanted "every bit of information available at the time," according to the admiral. In addition to seeing officials at the two bases, Admiral Grenfell personally called on Mrs. Harvey. Then, en route back to Washington, Secretary Korth and Admiral Grenfell flew out over the search area and talked to the search commander by radio.

Back in Washington, Admiral Anderson met the press again at 10:30 a.m. "This is a very sad occasion for me because very reluctantly I have come to the conclusion that the USS *Thresher,* which we have had for a time as missing has indeed been lost," he said. Then, telling of the oil slick, recovery of the plastic and cork debris, and failure to communicate with the *Thresher* in any way, Admiral Anderson explained: "So I conclude with great regret and sadness that this ship with 129 fine souls aboard is lost."

In reply to reporters' questions, the four-star admiral stated that Admiral Rickover had assured him that there was no danger of radioactivity from the *Thresher,* and that there were no Soviet or communist state-operated ships or submarines in the area.

It is worth noting that Admiral Anderson was asked: "Did the last message from the *Thresher* indicate that everything was proceeding normally?"

"Yes" was the response, and the questioning shifted to another theme.

By the time of the "Thank you, sir!" that traditionally ends most official Washington press conferences, no one who attended the session had the slightest doubt that the world's most advanced nuclear-powered submarine and all in her were lost.

In some ways it was ironic that Admiral Anderson was the Chief of Naval Operations at the time of the *Thresher* tragedy. Although a career naval aviator, Admiral Anderson had brought a broad outlook with him to the Navy's No. 1 job. In fact, he had become an outspoken supporter of nuclear-propelled submarines. When the *Thresher* was lost he was going over the head of the Secretary of Defense in urging the Congress to authorize more nuclear attack submarines. And it had been Admiral Anderson who announced that the Soviets definitely had nuclear-propelled submarines. In late 1961, Admiral Anderson said that the Soviets have "a limited number of nuclear-powered submarines." He added that the Soviets were probably having "some problems" with them and "it wouldn't surprise me if they lost some. We haven't lost any yet and don't intend to. . . ."

The Soviet Navy had completed its first nuclear submarine, the *K-3*, in 1958, less than four years after the USS *Nautilus*. No Soviet nuclear submarines had been lost to that time. But now the United States had lost a nuclear submarine—and it had lost its best.

On the morning of April 11, gale warnings were posted for the area where the *Thresher* had made her last dive. Seas running between six and ten feet, high winds, and scattered showers made an uncomfortable job still more uncomfortable.

More ships began joining the search force, among them the 210-foot *Atlantis II*. She was the most advanced oceanographic ship flying the American flag. Operated by the Woods Hole Oceanographic Institution, the *Atlantis II* had been sampling water and marine life in the Gulf of Maine. She was quickly loaned to the Navy so that her excellent depth-recording instruments could be used in the search for the *Thresher*.

Because the *Atlantis II* was on a chemical-biological cruise, her bottom-sounding gear was not fully operable. Woods Hole scientists and several hundred pounds of gear from the institution's laboratories near Cape Cod were placed on board the destroyer *Hazelwood* late on the afternoon of the 11th, and the warship headed to sea.

About noon that same day, the ships that were methodically searching the area where the *Thresher* went down began to recover additional debris believed to be from the lost submarine. The submarine rescue ship *Sunbird* picked up two rubber gloves. Oil samples, bits of cork and plastic, and a tube of "baker's flavoring," were transferred, along with the gloves, to the destroyer *Roberts,* which headed for Newport, Rhode Island, site of the inquiry into the *Thresher's* loss.

Coming the other way, the destroyer *Hazelwood* raced through rough seas during the night with the Woods Hole scientists and equipment. The *Hazelwood* and *Atlantis II* rendezvoused on the afternoon of April 12. The equipment was successfully transferred to the research ship as the two vessels steamed alongside each other, but it was judged too rough for the safe transfer of personnel. They were taken aboard the *Atlantis II* at dawn on the 13th, when the seas had calmed down.

In addition to her bottom-sounding gear, the *Atlantis II* was equipped to take samples of the ocean bottom. There had been much concern over the possible danger of radiation from the *Thresher's* nuclear power plant. Earlier Admiral Rickover had issued a public statement declaring: "I can assure you there is no radioactive hazard as a result of this unfortunate accident. Reactors of the type used in the *Thresher,* as well as in all our nuclear submarines and surface ships, can remain submerged indefinitely in seawater without creating any hazard."

Now bottom samples taken by the *Atlantis II* and tests of the debris recovered from the area showed no signs of abnormal radioactivity.

(Three days after the *Thresher* was lost, retired Soviet Admiral of the Fleet Ivan S. Isakov asserted: "The sinking of the newly charged atomic reactor is sure to contaminate the Atlantic waters, all the more so since the tragedy took place in the northern current of the Gulf Stream." Some Washington observers believed that the Soviet admiral's statement indicated that the Soviets had experienced contamination troubles with their own nuclear submarines.)

With her bottom-sounding gear in full operation, the *Atlantis II* began mapping the seafloor—looking for irregularities on the bottom that might be the remains of the *Thresher*. The Navy oceanographic research-and-survey ships *Allegheny, Chain, Conrad, Gilliss, Mission Capistrano, Prevail, Requisite,* and *Rockville* joined the *Atlantis II* in the hunt.

It was a frustrating hunt. A variety of objects on the ocean floor—old shipwrecks, large rock formations—would present the same image to the *Atlantis II*'s sounding gear as would the bulk of the *Thresher* if it were still mostly intact. Thus, suspect objects would have to be photographed by special deep-sea cameras before they could be intelligently identified.

By April 22, the search force, led by *Atlantis II*, had located about a dozen "objects" on the ocean floor in a 100-square-mile area where the *Thresher* went down. . . . "Half look like real good prospects," said a Navy spokesman at the time. But photographing the six protuberances that were "good prospects" involved a host of problems. When a "bump" is found on the ocean floor by ships tossing around on the surface of the rough Atlantic, 8,400 feet above, the protuberance can only be "pinpointed" to about a 100-yard circle. Then a camera must be lowered to photograph the suspect area. The camera rig, with its synchronized flash lamps to illuminate the dark depths, is lowered to the ocean floor almost a mile and a half down. Powerful currents swing the rig to and fro until the men on the surface are never quite sure of the exact position they are photographing. Lowering cameras and other instruments on a cable to a desired point on the ocean floor a mile and a half down had been compared by one oceanographer to "lowering a ping-pong ball into a beer can from the top of a three-story building while blindfolded and during a northeaster."

The big Edgerton underwater cameras—named after Dr. Harold Edgerton of the Massachusetts Institute of Technology—were mounted together with powerful strobe lights and sounding equipment and lowered to within 15 to 30 feet above the ocean floor. The ship towing the rig had to move slowly, a half-knot or a knot, depending on wind conditions. The cameras could take a sequence of about 500 photographs timed at eight-second intervals. At the end of the 500-shot sequence the camera had to be retrieved by slowly reeling in the mile and a half of cable. Then the film had to be extracted from the pressure case and developed. One scientist calculated that if the incredible happened and perfect pictures were taken for complete coverage with no overlapping, it would require more than 46,000 exposures to photograph a single square mile of the ocean floor.

It would be a long and tedious task at best; but a necessary one. The Navy had lost its most advanced undersea craft. The Navy had to do its best to find out why and to insure it did not happen again.

Once the remains of the *Thresher* could be pinpointed, the Navy's deep-diving bathyscaph *Trieste* could be sent down to visually investigate the hulk in hope of discovering the cause of the submarine's loss. The *Trieste* was able to dive to the deepest ocean depths. However, her horizontal search abilities were severely limited, her range being measured in yards. But once the unique craft is over an object on the ocean floor the men in the *Trieste* could observe it, take photographs, and possibly poke at it with a remote-control pickup arm (see Chapter 7).

Thus, hour after hour, day after day, the search for the *Thresher*'s remains continued.

Because of the difficulties in identifying the protuberances on the ocean floor, in early May the Navy decided to sink another submarine in the search area so that sonar could follow her down and give a "picture" of what a submarine on the bottom looked like. Also, by following the submarine down the Navy could learn how the local ocean currents affected a falling object the size of the *Thresher*. On April 26 an old automobile had been sunk in the area as a metallic target for sonar equipment. However, the car had turned during its fall and drifted out of the sonar beam that was trying to follow it to the ocean floor.

The submarine selected to follow the *Thresher* to a watery grave was the *Toro*. She also was built at the Portsmouth yard, but in only six and a half months during the around-the-clock, assembly-line days of 1944. She was 311 feet, 8 inches—33 feet, 2 inches longer than the *Thresher*. But the *Toro* was built for "fast" (20-knot) surface running. Underwater she could make only a few knots—at most ten for a few minutes—on her battery. Her narrow hull displaced only 1,570 tons in comparison to the 3,500 tons of the *Thresher*, whose fish-shaped hull was capable of moving half again as fast underwater as the *Toro* could on the surface. But the old *Toro* would make an adequate sonar target.

A month before the *Thresher* was lost the *Toro* was decommissioned at Philadelphia. Too old and too slow, she was replaced in the front line by a newer nuclear boat. The *Toro* was to have been used as a target for new weapons. She was instead fitted out as a giant sonar reflector, and preparations were made for the *Toro* to be towed to the search area and sunk under "controlled conditions" on May 20 or 21.

But suddenly plans to sink the *Toro* were halted. In mid-May the photographs being taken of the ocean floor began revealing numerous small objects in the area where the *Thresher* was lost—bits of paper, small wires, small metallic objects, and other items classified as "trash." Officials were cautious in their estimates of the importance of the objects: "No readily identifiable objects are shown," and "It has not been confirmed that these small objects are from the submarine *Thresher*." But there was a possibility.

As the *Atlantis II* and *Conrad* towed deep-water cameras, others methods of search were being conducted for the *Thresher*. The research ship *Conrad* also used drag lines in an effort to grapple debris from the lost submarine—and possibly the sunken craft herself. On May 27, the *Conrad*'s dredge brought to the surface 19 small packages of "O" rings. These are washer-like rubber rings, the size of a nickel or quarter, that are used as seals in various types of hydraulic equipment in a ship.

Each of the envelopes and each of the small "O" rings was imprinted with stock numbers and other data that could be traced. The 19 packages could be divided into three categories, six in one, six in another, and seven in the third. A number of Navy ships, including the *Thresher*, could have carried the packages in the first category. The "O" rings in the second category could be traced to two ships—the *Thresher* and a destroyer. In the third category, there was only one possible craft—the *Thresher*.

With "almost a 100 per cent certainty," the rings were from the *Thresher*, according to a Navy spokesman. It was a discovery of great importance, for until then nothing found could be traced directly and only to the *Thresher*. The gloves, pieces of plastic and cork, and oil samples recovered were believed to be from the *Thresher*, but there was no definite identification as there was through the stock numbers of the "O" rings and their envelopes.

On the heels of the "O" ring discovery, the *Conrad*'s deepwater cameras took photos of "wreckage" on the bottom of the search area. On the afternoon of May 30, the *Conrad*'s developed film was believed to show the *Thresher*'s sail, a diving plane, and a portion of the craft's hull. Eight of the 500 sequence shots on the film roll reportedly photographed portions of the *Thresher*.

Dr. Joseph Lamar Worzel, assistant director of Lamont Geological Observatory of Columbia University in New York, was the senior scientist on board the *Conrad*. He had long experience in underwater photography, including the photographing of submarines.

As the *Conrad* steamed back to port with the photographs that were believed to show wreckage of the *Thresher*, Dr. Worzel called Washington and spoke with Captain Frank Andrews, Dr. Arthur Maxwell of the Office of Naval Research, and Captain Charles B. Bishop of Naval Operations' Undersea Warfare Development Division. A commercial radio circuit was being used, and there was no actual reference to the *Thresher* or even the *Conrad* in the conversation.

"Dr. Worzel said preliminary examination of the photos indicated we had found what we were looking for," Dr. Maxwell recalled later. After the cryptic radio-telephone conversation, the three men in Washington decided to alert top Navy leaders that it was believed the *Thresher* had been found.

On the basis of the reports from the *Conrad,* Secretary of the Navy Fred Korth told a news conference the next day: "There has been a submarine determined to be the *Thresher* located on the ocean floor with a rupture in the hull." Captain Bishop, a submarine specialist, explained that the best information available indicated the entire hull of the submarine had been found. But he added: "Of course this is based on only the eight pictures of one part of the hull as the camera moves across it."

The bathyscaph *Trieste* was made ready at Boston to be towed out to sea to make dives where the *Conrad* had taken the photographs. It was estimated that the *Trieste* would make a dive over the "wreckage" about June 10 if the weather was favorable.

Elation over the *Conrad*'s photographs was short-lived. The *Conrad* quickly returned to port with the photographs, and on the night of May 31 they were flown to Washington for expert examination at the Naval Photographic Interpretation Center in Anacostia in eastern Washington, D.C. The next day a Navy spokesman sadly announced that the photos definitely did not show the *Thresher.* "None [of the objects in the photos] could be identified as being any part of the *Thresher,*" the Navy said. In fact, it appeared the camera had actually taken a series of pictures of part of the camera rig itself.

The rig containing the camera was lowered along a steel cable anchored to the seafloor. As the camera neared the bottom of the cable, it turned around and made a fast-sequence series of eight pictures, which actually showed the cable anchor partially imbedded in the silt of the ocean floor. The lead weight's outline was mistaken for part of the *Thresher*'s hull and superstructure. The proximity of the camera to the anchor falsely enlarged the image. This, coupled with rips in the film's emulsion that gave the appearance of a rupture in the submarine's hull, caused Dr. Worzel to make the false assumption.

The Navy was now back where it had been seven weeks earlier except that there was reasonable evidence—the "O" ring find—that the *Thresher* had indeed broken open or possibly disintegrated.

The error in interpreting the photographs and failure to locate the *Thresher*'s remains caused the Navy to re-evaluate its efforts to find the submarine. The preparations to send the bathyscaph *Trieste* to sea were halted "until more positive evidence of the exact location of the *Thresher* is known." And again came the monotonous work of photographing the ocean floor, probing the depths with sonar, and attempting to detect metal in the ocean-bottom silt with magnetic detection devices.

The washout of the photos taken on May 30 caused a letdown within the Navy. Indeed, the searchers began asking whether the *Thresher* could ever be found. Had she disintegrated as she plunged into the depths where the pressure is thousands of pounds on every square inch of hull surface? Was she buried in the silt of the ocean floor? Had the *Thresher*'s speed and momentum as she plunged to the bottom carried her miles away from where she was thought to be?

The search continued.

Then, in mid-June, the oceanographic research ship *Conrad,* under the direction of Dr. Worzel, made some "highly significant" photographs of debris on the ocean floor in the search area. The objects were identified as an air bottle "similar to that carried aboard Navy ships," a section of broken pipe, a piece of metal plate approximately eight feet by nine feet with perforated metal and insulating material attached similar to that used in submarine construction, a brush some 13 inches long, and a ladle or large spoon.

The Navy announcement of the debris was notably cautious. According to photographic interpreters, the pictures of the debris "could not be definitely correlated with the *Thresher*." However, the Navy was so encouraged by the photographs that it was decided to send the bathyscaph *Trieste* down to look more closely and investigate the area. The *Toro* sinking was now postponed indefinitely.

Man was again going down to the 8,400-foot ocean floor, but this time safely, in the Navy's "inner space" ship.

CHAPTER 7

FINDING THE *THRESHER*

As the stricken *Thresher* plummeted toward the bottom of the ocean she was soon beyond the reach of any existing rescue device or manned U.S. submersible—with one exception. The Navy bathyscaph *Trieste* was the world's only manned vehicle that could penetrate the 8,400-feet depths. In fact, the *Trieste* had dived to more than four times that depth in the Pacific in January of 1960, reaching a depth of 35,800 feet in the Marianas Trench, the deepest known point of the oceans.

On the morning after the *Thresher* was lost, Admiral Anderson announced that the *Trieste* would be brought across the continent and made ready to investigate the sunken *Thresher* "if it can be found."

The *Trieste*, the Navy's only bathyscaph (the term derived from the Greek words *bathy* and *scaphos* meaning "deep boat"), was essentially a float-like 34,000-gallon gasoline tank with an observation gondola attached beneath her "hull." Because gasoline is lighter than water, the *Trieste* floated, aided by two air tanks mounted at either end of the gasoline float. To submerge, these tanks were flooded with sea water. To resurface, operators simply released two tubs of steel BB shot held inside the float. Because pressure inside the float was equal to the seawater outside, there was no danger of collapse. The gondola below the float held the normal crew of two men—three could be squeezed in—and a variety of scientific equipment. (After the *Thresher* search operation, the *Trieste* was shipped back to the West Coast where she was rebuilt to give her more underwater speed and maneuverability, becoming the *Trieste II*.)

Described as "the world's longest elevator," the *Trieste* was essentially an up-and-down vehicle. Once at her operating depth during the search, the *Trieste* had three small, battery-powered electric motors that propelled her at about 1½ miles-per-hour for four hours. The *Trieste* also carried four external 35-millimeter cameras that could take up to 2,000 pictures and a sonar that could probe about 400 yards.

The United States purchased the 50-ton *Trieste* from her designer and builder, Professor Auguste Piccard, in 1958, primarily for research in "inner space," the depths of the world's oceans. But, according to one official Navy publication, the *Trieste* was also wanted to "examine possible naval uses for this type of craft, such as a submarine rescue vessel or a deep-diving submarine and other devices."

There could be no rescue for the stricken *Thresher*. But the *Trieste* could carry engineers into the depths to look over the submarine's remains, if they could be found. Because of the craft's limited horizontal mobility the *Thresher's* hulk would have to be pinpointed before the *Trieste* could dive.

Immediately after the *Thresher's* loss the Navy began making plans for moving the *Trieste* to the East Coast. The possibilities of flying the bathyscaph to the East Coast or bringing her across country by train were considered, but quickly discarded. It was found more feasible to move the *Trieste* by ship.

At San Diego—the *Trieste*'s home port—the bathyscaph was carefully loaded aboard the dock landing ship *Point Defiance*. The *Point Defiance* was especially designed to transport landing craft in a large "docking well," which could be flooded to enable landing craft to drive in or out. The *Trieste* fitted easily into the big ship's well.

While the *Point Defiance* sailed toward Boston via the Panama Canal with her unusual cargo, the *Trieste*'s skipper, Lieutenant Commander Donald Keach, flew to Washington to confer with the *Thresher* search directors. In Washington, Keach explained that once the *Thresher* was located the *Trieste* could move in close to the submarine's remains for observation.

The *Point Defiance* delivered the *Trieste* to Boston on April 26 and Navymen hurried to make the craft fully operable. The *Trieste* was towed to sea and made a brief test dive to a depth of 702 feet some 60 nautical miles off Boston on May 5. With Commander Keach at her controls, the *Trieste* dived to check out equipment and was then towed back to Boston and held on standby, ready to go to sea within 24 hours.

When the research ship *Conrad* reported photographing the *Thresher*'s remains on May 30, the Navy announced "plans are being laid to move her [the *Trieste*] out as early as possible. . . ." June 10, depending on the weather, was predicted as "a good date" for the *Trieste* to make her first dive. But these plans were halted two days later when it was found that the *Conrad*'s photographs showed the underwater camera's anchor and not the remains of the *Thresher*.

Then, on June 19, the Navy announced that the *Trieste* would conduct "exploratory dives in an attempt to locate the hulk of the nuclear submarine USS *Thresher*." She would dive in the area where photographs of the ocean floor had revealed heavy debris, including the air bottle, broken pipe, and metal plates.

The salvage ship *Preserver* took the *Trieste* in tow at a speed of about four knots and headed east for the *Thresher* search area. The dock landing ship *Fort Snelling* went along to provide support facilities for the small bathyscaph.

The *Fort Snelling* and the *Preserver,* the latter with the *Trieste* trailing behind at the end of a towline, reached the search area on the morning of June 23. That afternoon the *Fort Snelling* launched a 50-foot landing craft called a "mike boat." This small craft would serve as a communications link with the *Trieste* when the bathyscaph submerged. No wires or cables would connect the *Trieste* to the surface when she went down—only the invisible sound impulses of her underwater telephone or UQC. Next the search ship *Conrad* floated a doughnut-shaped buoy to serve as a "lighthouse" for the *Trieste.* The buoy—placed near where the *Thresher* made her last dive and above where the debris had been photographed—served as a float for electronic devices that would give the *Trieste* a point of reference for her dives to the ocean floor.

While the ships were going about their work, the Soviet tanker *Pokyeatan* passed through the search area, coming within 700 yards of the *Conrad.* She was a fuel and water carrier that usually served Soviet fishing trawlers. The *Pokyeatan* dipped her flag as a courtesy. The *Fort Snelling* signaled her: "I am engaged in submarine survey work. You should stand clear of me." To this the *Pokyeatan* made no reply, but moved off to the south. During the next few days more Soviet craft would sail through the area, apparently looking over the special-purpose U.S. ships.

On the morning of June 24 the *Trieste* prepared for her first operational dive in the Atlantic. Previously, the unique craft had operated only in the Mediterranean Sea and Pacific Ocean. There was the shallow dive off Boston to check out her equipment, but this was the first deep dive in the Atlantic.

A small boat put Commander Keach and civilian scientist Kenneth Mackenzie aboard the *Trieste*. Mackenzie was a senior scientist at the Navy Electronics Laboratory at San Diego, the organization that operated the *Trieste*. They would make the first dive in search of the *Thresher*. Lieutenant George Martin, second in command of the bathyscaph, and Giuseppe Buono, the craft's engineer, were already aboard making ready for the dive. Several Navy frogmen also assisted in the preparations.

Keach and Mackenzie descended the access tube in the *Trieste*'s float and entered the cramped, sphere-like gondola below. Equipment was given a last-minute check.

A few minutes after 10 o'clock, an outboard motorboat took Martin and Buono off the low-lying *Trieste*. The end tanks of the bathyscaph's float were flooded with seawater. Ordinarily, this reduces the craft's buoyancy so that she begins to descend. But because of the choppy surface—which provided an upward lift on the *Trieste*—she did not go down.

From inside the craft Keach requested by underwater telephone that Martin and Buono use the "beanbag" technique. The outboard boat from the *Preserver* came close in to the *Trieste,* and Buono began tossing 22-pound bags of ballast onto the bathyscaph's deck. Still the *Trieste* was reluctant to plunge into the depths. Indeed, it was as if the craft feared a fate awaited her like that which befell the *Thresher.*

The outboard had to return to the *Preserver* for more ballast bags to toss on the *Trieste*'s deck. Meanwhile, from within the bathyscaph, Keach detected a loose rubber tubing on the craft and called for frogmen to fix it. Two scuba divers quickly swam over, clambered onto the *Trieste's* deck, and secured the tubing.

Suddenly, the *Trieste* gave up her battle to stay on the surface and began to disappear into the choppy waters, leaving only the bobbing heads of the Navy frogmen. Slowly, the *Trieste* began the hour-long descent to ocean floor, 8,400 feet below. It was 10:35 a.m.

Those aboard the *Preserver, Fort Snelling,* and *Conrad* waited. While the *Trieste* was down the Soviet fishing trawler *Penhtop* appeared on the horizon, heading on a course that would take her to within a mile of the buoy marking the site of the *Trieste's* dive. In response to signals from the *Trieste's* support ships, the trawler altered course and moved off.

Once on the bottom, the *Trieste* carefully searched the ocean floor for debris of the *Thresher.* An electronic signal from the marker buoy could not be detected and the navigational capabilities of the *Trieste* were somewhat hampered. She went down a little farther east than had been planned. Then, hovering some 40 feet above the sea bottom, the *Trieste* searched about two square miles.

At 2:30 p.m. the *Trieste* signaled she was beginning her ascent, and an hour and 25 minutes later she broke the surface. An official summary released shortly after the dive said "nothing of significance was noted." In describing the craft's first dive in search of the *Thresher,* on-scene-commander Captain Andrews noted it was "extremely satisfactory from an operational point of view." He also noted the electronic signal failure that restricted the *Trieste's* navigational abilities.

For the next morning's dive, Lieutenant Martin would be the pilot and Mackenzie would again serve as observer. But at 11 a.m. the next day it was decided to postpone the second dive for 24 hours. There were several reasons for the delay—

the faulty electronic signal in the buoy; the need for recharging the *Trieste*'s batteries; and the night before Martin had sprained his ankle while transferring from a small boat to the *Trieste*. Officials felt it was better that he not be kept confined in the tight quarters of the *Trieste*. (When Martin was injured, Commander Keach immediately made plans to operate the *Trieste* on her second dive, but because of the other problems it was decided to wait another day.)

Thus, on the morning of June 26 the *Trieste* submerged again, manned by Martin and Mackenzie. This was a six-hour dive—an hour down, four hours on the bottom, and an hour coming up; the limit of the *Trieste*'s endurance.

In landing on the ocean floor, the bathyscaph settled about two feet into the soft silt-clay bottom. To avoid dropping too much ballast to get clear of the bottom and thus aborting the dive, Martin tried to work the *Trieste* clear of the silt with the craft's three electric motors. Martin intended to take the *Trieste* up 40 feet. Instead, the momentum of working loose carried the *Trieste* up some 480 feet above the ocean floor.

While Martin struggled to regain control of the *Trieste*, the craft's sonar picked up a metallic object estimated to be about 60 feet long. The sonar contact lasted about two minutes. But, as the *Trieste* returned to the bottom, Martin was unable to re-establish the sonar contact. The contact was placed within the 250-by-2,700-yard area where the greatest concentration of debris had been photographed. (Three magnetic contacts had also been made by the *Conrad* in this same area.) After being unable to find the object, Martin brought the *Trieste* to the surface.

The next day—June 27—the *Trieste* again went down, this time operated by Keach and Mackenzie. While the *Trieste* was preparing to dive another Soviet trawler-support ship passed through the area. This was the third Soviet ship observed in the search area in the past five days, despite U.S. requests that all shipping avoid the area while search operations were in progress. Garbage and other objects thrown from a passing ship could conceivably damage the submerged *Trieste* and, should the bathyscaph suddenly bound to the surface and collide with a passing ship, there could be a major disaster.

Down the *Trieste* went into the cold, dark depths of the Atlantic in search of the 60-foot object her sonar had found the day before. On the bottom the *Trieste* found a yellow rubber shoe cover, one of a pair usually worn by crewmen in nuclear submarines when they enter the reactor compartment to prevent radioactive dust from being picked up by the men's shoes and carried to other parts of the submarine. The "bootee"—in a folded position on the sea bottom—had the letters "SSN" stenciled on it, the Navy designation for attack nuclear submarines. A figure, spaced a little to the right of the lettering and clearly legible, was a "5," the first digit of the *Thresher's* hull number, SSN 593. The rest of the numbers were hidden because the bootee was folded. Since such bootees are never jettisoned, but are put in a special disposal bag at the entrance to the reactor compartment, the one on the ocean floor could not have come from an intact submarine. In addition to the bootee, "a massive concentration" of paper and lightweight debris was observed, according to Commander Keach.

While the *Trieste* was down, still another Soviet ship steamed into the search area. Identified as the large fishing trawler/factory ship *Kurpin,* she came some four hours after the previous Soviet ship and passed within 200 yards of the *Fort Snelling,* again ignoring the earlier requests that all shipping stay 25 nautical miles away during diving operations.

The *Trieste* returned to the surface without locating the object her sonar had picked up the day before. But search officials were highly encouraged by the discovery of the bootee. "It could have come from the *Thresher*," Captain Andrews said cautiously. But there was still disappointment over failure to find more remains of the *Thresher*.

The *Trieste* made her fourth dive on June 29, manned by Martin, Mackenzie, and an additional observer, Lieutenant Commander Eugene J. Cash, assigned to Captain Andrews' search operations staff. As the *Trieste* cruised along the sea floor, her observers sighted two craters in the ocean bottom. One measured about 15 feet deep and 40 feet across. The second—a couple of feet away—was estimated at 200 feet across and 40 feet deep. Photographs were taken of the two holes. They were discovered as the *Trieste* followed a "trail" of debris that included scraps of metal and paper and the yellow bootee which had been located previously.

Back the *Trieste* went to the surface with her prized photographs of the craters. The holes were said to be "quite near" the spot where a compressed air bottle similar to those used in nuclear submarines had been photographed earlier in the month.

Officials cautioned that the holes might have been part of the natural topography of the ocean floor. Captain Andrews noted that there was no mounding of silt around the edges of the holes, such as would naturally occur if any object had been driven into the ocean floor with great force.

The fifth dive was scheduled for the next day. Three men made the June 30 dive—Captain Andrews, who was celebrating his 42nd birthday, Keach, and Mackenzie. But on this dive the *Trieste* was hampered by mechanical difficulties: A gyrocompass failure made it impossible to navigate accurately, and one of the craft's three small propulsion motors failed, reducing her mobility. The gyrocompass "failure" was caused when someone inside the cramped gondola inadvertently pushed against the gyrocompass switch, turning the device off. Although the trouble was quickly discovered, the gyrocompass could not provide accurate readings until it was reset, which would mean surfacing and aligning it with the operating compass of a surface ship.

The *Trieste* spent only two hours and nine minutes on the bottom and then headed back up. In all, she was underwater a total of four hours and 45 minutes on this fifth dive. Though the results were disappointing, even the failure to find anything significant helped to define the limits of the debris.

On the next day, July 1, the *Preserver* began towing the *Trieste* back to Boston for repairs and a checkup. Most of the small task force that had supported her also headed into port, leaving the research ship *Gibbs*, which stayed on to continue a bottom search of the area with underwater cameras and sonar.

But the *Trieste*'s search did reveal something possibly of great value: the two ocean-bottom craters. After the *Thresher* was lost on April 10, some Navymen and scientists theorized that the submarine could have filled with water, fallen backward, and then, like a falling bomb, plunged into the sea floor at more than 100 miles-per-hour. One calculation had the water-filled submarine reaching 125 miles-per-hour when she hit the ocean floor. Falling perfectly vertical with her stern pointing down, some calculations indicated, the *Thresher* could have smashed into the ocean floor and gone down some 500 feet into the sediment. This would put the highest point of the 278½-foot *Thresher* about 220 feet below the ocean floor and leave a crater like that found by the *Trieste*. The smaller crater nearby might have been caused by a part of the submarine breaking off just before she hit the bottom.

Others who studied the *Thresher* disaster felt that the submarine could not have slammed into the ocean bottom at such great velocity and buried herself. To do so the submarine would have had to fall straight down without breaking up. The fact that so much debris, apparently from the *Thresher,* had been located indicated that the submarine broke up as she sank, thus causing drag, slowing her descent, and lessening the impact on the ocean floor.

Upon her return to Boston the *Trieste* was given a careful inspection, and preparations were made for performing minor repairs, adjustments, and modifications after her exposure to the depths of the Atlantic. The welds on the *Trieste's* float-like hull, the straps securing her crew-equipment gondola, and all the craft's equipment were checked and tested. A remote-control, mechanical pickup arm was also hooked up on the *Trieste's* forward ballast hopper during the yard period. The device, which could be controlled from inside the gondola, was designed to pick up objects from the ocean floor, but so far had never worked properly. It did not work during the first series of dives because the limited number of openings in the *Trieste's* gondola were needed for strain gauges to measure the effect of pressure on the craft, and were not available for the pickup-arm control wires. The *Trieste* was to remain at Boston for some six weeks before returning to the *Thresher* search area.

While the *Trieste* was being readied for the next series of dives, other facets of the search continued as oceanographic research ships criss-crossed the search area with underwater cameras and electronic and magnetic detectors. The Navy oceanographic tug *Allegheny* dropped 1,441 "signposts" on the ocean floor in the search area to help guide the *Trieste*. These "signposts," colored, plastic discs attached to weighted nylon cords, were placed in 11 rows at intervals of about 60 feet. The rows—approximately 750 feet apart—formed avenues on the ocean floor in a generally north-south direction that could help guide the *Trieste* as she ambled along searching for the *Thresher*. Each of the markers, dubbed "fortune cookies" by the Navymen who handled them, was numbered and color-coded.

Also in the search area, the research ship *Gibbs* rigged and planted on the surface buoys that would serve as electronic landmarks for the *Trieste*. This work by the *Gibbs* climaxed 24 days on station in the search area using a variety of scientific devices to plot the ocean floor.

Back at Boston, the *Trieste* made a brief trim dive to check her equilibrium, sonar, underwater lights, communications, and propulsion system. Then, on the afternoon of August 15, the *Preserver* headed out to sea with the *Trieste* in tow. A couple of hours later, the faster dock landing ship *Fort Snelling* left Boston on the same heading.

On the 17th, the research ship *Gilliss* arrived in the search area and began checking the exact position of the navigation buoys planted earlier. As the *Preserver* and *Trieste* neared the search area, Lieutenant Commander Keach and his crew prepared the bathyscaph for the first dive in the new series of six to ten dives, which was tentatively scheduled for Monday, August 19, weather permitting.

But there was no dive on the 19th. One of the navigation buoys had drifted; then problems set in with the electronic navigation equipment on the ships; and then bad weather caused a series of delays.

Finally, on August 23, the *Trieste* plunged into the depths in search of the *Thresher*. Keach piloted her on the dive, and Mackenzie of the Navy Electronics Laboratory served as observer.

Because of fog on the surface, the dive was delayed until late in the day. Once underwater the *Trieste*'s descent was slowed because of the difficulty in penetrating a cold-water layer at 200 feet, and the crew also discovered that the *Trieste*'s navigation equipment was not functioning properly. So, after only an hour and 15 minutes on the bottom, the bathyscaph began to head back up to the surface. However, the dive was not a total failure, for the *Trieste* located one of the plastic markers planted earlier by the *Allegheny*. The number "45" on the white disc was clearly visible to both Keach and Mackenzie.

Again and again poor weather prevented the *Trieste* from returning to the depths. An attempt was made to provide a sheltered area for the *Trieste* to dive in by having the *Fort Snelling* take station on the windward side, but this didn't work. Then, as word came that Hurricane Beulah might be heading into the search area, the *Fort Snelling* and *Preserver*, the *Trieste* in tow, began steaming north toward Shelburne, Nova Scotia, to escape the storm. The *Gilliss* remained in the search area to continue her underwater photography work, but always ready to run for cover should Beulah veer into the area.

When it became certain that Beulah would not endanger ships in the search area, the *Fort Snelling* and *Preserver*—with the *Trieste* trailing behind—turned back. Valuable time had been lost, and Beulah was a warning of the kind of weather to be expected in the North Atlantic during the coming fall.

The *Trieste* made her second dive of the series on August 27, but there were "no significant findings." Lieutenant Martin piloted the bathyscaph on this trip to the bottom, accompanied by Mackenzie and Lieutenant Commander A.H. Gilmore, operations officer on the staff of the search commander. This time a red plastic marker with the number "32" on it was sighted during the craft's three hours and 25 minutes on the ocean floor.

Three more dives followed as the weather remained relatively favorable. On August 28, Keach, Gilmore, and Commander J.W. Davies of the Navy Electronics Laboratory, were on the bottom for three hours and 40 minutes; on the 29th, Martin, Davies, and Lieutenant Commander A.D. James, a submarine medical officer, were on the bottom for some four hours; and on September 1, Keach, James, and Lieutenant E.E. Henifin of the search force staff were on the sea floor for an hour and 40 minutes. The fifth and last dive was cut short by a partial battery failure in the *Trieste*.

The Navy made no announcements of what was found on these dives. The *Trieste* and her support ships *Preserver* and *Fort Snelling* returned to Boston, arriving there on September 4. That night Captain Andrews and Lieutenant Commander Keach flew down to Washington. A few minutes before noon the following day, the nation's top military reporters, alerted that "something big" was coming off, were handed press releases as they stood waiting for a noon press briefing in the Pentagon. The release—with the familiar blue Department of Defense letterhead—announced "the location of structural parts of the *Thresher* on the ocean floor [have] been positively confirmed by the bathyscaph *Trieste*" and "the associated operational aspects of the search for the nuclear submarine *Thresher* [are being] terminated."

The search was over.

Secretary of the Navy Korth, Vice Admiral Ramage (who had led an early phase of the *Thresher* search and was now Deputy

Chief of Naval Operations for Fleet Operations and Readiness), Captain Andrews, Lieutenant Commander Keach, and Dr. Maxwell faced a battery of television cameras, microphones, and reporters.

Prominently displayed on a table before them was a section of pipe 57 inches long. Attached to the pipe were a section of sheet metal, bits of lagging, and a rusty bracket. The sheet of metal was caked with white oxidation. The pipe was grotesquely twisted. It was part of the *Thresher*.

Secretary Korth read a statement to the newsmen recounting the highlights of the five-month search for the *Thresher*. He described briefly the recovery of the copper pipe by the *Trieste* on her August 28 dive, the discovery of other parts of the *Thresher,* and announced the termination of the search.

Then the others stood before the cameras and answered questions. Commander Keach, who had seen the "structural parts" of the *Thresher* and had brought one of them back to the surface, was the target for most of the questions. He was the man. In the press room, later at a local television station, and that evening with the author of this book, Keach described the remains of the *Thresher*.

"The ocean floor in the area is like an automobile junkyard," he explained. He told of guiding the bathyscaph through the debris-covered area, taking care not to bump any of the sections of twisted steel that were scattered about.

Commander Keach decided to try and bring to the surface one of the pieces of the *Thresher* with the *Trieste's* mechanical pickup arm. "I've never been able to use it to pick up anything before—not even a starfish," he said. But on the August 28 dive he was determined to bring back a piece of the *Thresher*.

"There were dozens of pieces—some up to 20 feet long. It was difficult to decide what to bring up. I considered trying to loop the pickup arm through a large piece of debris, but decided not to try it after all," Keach said.

Sizes of objects are difficult to determine while underwater, he explained, adding that he wanted to avoid striking debris with the bathyscaph. There was also a chance that the bathyscaph—with her three-man crew—might become ensnared in the debris and be anchored to the bottom. "We didn't want that to happen," Keach said.

After 15 minutes of manipulating the remote-control pickup arm, Keach managed to hook onto the section of copper pipe, which weighed about ten pounds.

"I chose it because there were appendages hanging from it, lagging insulation, and connections, and it was bent. I thought that if the arm's grip lost it on the way up some of the appendages might catch on the arm and hold it." With his prize Keach slowly brought the *Trieste* back to the surface, the ascent taking an hour and 55 minutes.

The pipe was identified as coming from inside of the *Thresher* and having been part of the air filtration system for the submarine's galley. Several job and serial numbers had been imprinted on the pipe with an electric-vibrator drill, along with the designation "593 boat."

Commander Keach also told of sighting and photographing a large piece of metal with the digits 0, 3, and 4 clearly visible. The numbers appeared to be draft markings, which are located on the forward and after end of a submarine's hull. Other items sighted included a hatch cover, battery plates, brackets, copper tubing, perforated aluminum sheets, and portions of the sonar equipment that had been housed in the *Thresher's* bow.

No human remains were sighted.

The *Trieste's* discoveries during her second series of dives in search of the *Thresher* established that the submarine had at least partially disintegrated, scattering debris over a wide area of the ocean floor. Because of the large amount of battery plate lying in the area, the early finding of material used in the reactor shielding, and recovery of a pipe from the galley, there was a possibility that the main portion of the hull may have broken open or even split in half amidships, scattering debris from that area of the submarine. Or, the tremendous pressure of the depths could have caused the *Thresher* to implode and disintegrate.

But the examination of the remainder of what had been the *Thresher* would have to wait. The second series of dives by the *Trieste* was delayed repeatedly because of winter weather setting into the North Atlantic. In addition, the ten-year-old *Trieste* was in need of extensive yard work. A new float—which would allow faster towing and increased range underwater—was being prepared for the *Trieste* on the West Coast. The skin of the float, only about three or four millimeters thick, had suffered from corrosion and fatigue, prompting the Navy to end the search.

Work of a strictly oceanographic nature, it was explained at the September 5 press conference, would continue in the area where the *Thresher* was lost, and as new deep-submergence craft became available, they could be employed in later search—and possibly even recovery operations—"if it proves feasible."

But the real search had ended. For Captain Andrews and Commander Keach, there were Navy Commendation Medals for their leadership in the search operation. For Dr. Maxwell, there was the Superior Civilian Achievement Award for directing the scientific steering committee of the search.

For the remains of the *Thresher*, there were the cold, dark depths which would serve as a crypt for the nothingness that had been 129 men.

CHAPTER 8

THE INQUIRY

"We have appointed a court of inquiry headed by one of our senior admirals, Vice Admiral Austin, the President of the Naval War College, assisted by other experienced submarine officers, to conduct an inquiry."

Thus, the same day that the *Thresher* was lost, Admiral Anderson announced the formal investigation into history's worst submarine disaster. The court of inquiry, which began on April 13, would hear testimony, look at exhibits, examine documents, and attempt to find the reason or reasons that the *Thresher* and all who were in her died.

The court's conclusions would include recommendations. But the court could not order any changes in policy or operations. It could not find anyone "guilty," yet it could—and some say did—send a man out of its portals broken so far as his naval career was concerned.

Five submarine officers were named to sit on the court. Vice Admiral Bernard Austin, who was to head the court, was president of the Naval War College, the Navy's highest professional school for officers. Admiral Austin was no novice to investigations of disaster. Two years earlier he had served as president of the court that investigated the fire that ravaged the unfinished aircraft carrier *Constellation* at the New York Naval Shipyard. Fifty men, all civilian shipyard workers, had died in that tragedy.

Named to serve with Admiral Austin on the *Thresher* inquiry were Rear Admiral Lawrence Daspit, who had seen action in the Pacific as a sub skipper during World War II and later commanded the Atlantic Fleet Submarine Force; Captain James Osborn, the first commanding officer of the first Polaris missile submarine, the *George Washington*; Captain William Hushing, the senior Navy representative at the commercial Electric Boat submarine yard; and Captain Norman Nash, commander of Service Squadron 8, a force of specialized fleet-support ships. By almost any definition of the term, these men were "experts" in the submarine business.

Because it was a naval court of inquiry, the panel would follow carefully laid out rules of order. Cocked hats and swords were not part of the uniform of the court, but they would not have been out of place in the formal and somber atmosphere. To insure that the prescribed rules and regulations were adhered to, and to pass judgment on legal technicalities, Captain Saul Katz, a law specialist, was named counsel for the court.

Admiral Austin opened the first session of the court at the New London Submarine Base, the *Thresher's* home port (although she had spent more time in Portsmouth), and the headquarters for the deputy commander of the Atlantic Fleet Submarine Force.

The court met briefly at New London and then moved to the Portsmouth Naval Shipyard, where the *Thresher* had been built, was later overhauled, and from where she had finally sailed on her last voyage. The Portsmouth yard had launched its first ship in 1814 and later became the leading government-owned submarine yard in the nation. The design work for the *Thresher* class submarines was done at Portsmouth, and several of the *Thresher's* sisterships were under construction there.

First witness before the court's initial session at Portsmouth was Commander Dean Axene. He was the first of the two men who had command of the *Thresher* and had been responsible for everyone and everything in her. The second commanding officer was now dead.

Commander Axene, asked for his opinion of the *Thresher's* fate, said: "There is no way for me or anyone else to know what happened out there, but it must have been associated with a flooding-type casualty. And the flooding would have been almost instantaneous, leaving such short time that the personnel could not react to let someone know they were in trouble."

He also testified about the *Thresher's* first deep-water dive, which was carried out under his command almost two years earlier. This dive—in the same area where the *Thresher* was lost—had to be halted suddenly because of trouble with instruments in the submarine. Commander Axene said the trouble was with the instruments and not the submarine herself. The dive, he related, "was to have been the first of the deeper dives of the *Thresher,* but before we reached our maximum depth point the instruments indicated something was wrong. The instruments were contradictory and I terminated the test before the deep diving was completed." He noted that he would have given the submarine a rating of "outstanding and excellent" after the instruments were corrected.

Giving his opinion of the *Thresher*-class submarines, Commander Axene told the court that after traveling some 30,000 miles, mostly submerged, and having undergone innumerable tests, he would evaluate the *Thresher* as "the best attack class submarine our Navy has produced." He said there were no major deficiencies and that some minor ones were known even before the *Thresher* was commissioned. These, he added, included the hydraulic system, the sonar equipment, and radio antenna. All were corrected.

For one hour and twenty minutes, Commander Axene talked and answered questions. What he said brought agreeing nods from the submarine and shipyard officers in the room. The *Thresher* had been a good ship manned by good men.

What the next witnesses had to say shocked the court.

On Saturday afternoon, following Commander Axene's testimony, Lieutenant (junior grade) James Watson gave his account of the *Thresher's* trials the morning of April 10. As the navigator and first lieutenant of the rescue ship *Skylark*, he had heard the *Thresher's* last messages.

Lieutenant Watson described the messages, including the phrases "have positive up angle" and "attempting to blow up," which he had heard over the *Skylark's* UQC underwater telephone on the morning of April 10. He told of the sounds of air being blown under high pressure and then sounds that Lieutenant Watson recognized as those of "a ship breaking up—like a compartment collapsing." In his words, "a muted dull thud." During World War II he had heard the sounds a ship makes when she breaks up, and he was sure of what he heard.

Lieutenant Watson differed with the *Skylark's* official log on the details of those last messages heard from the *Thresher*. Roy Mowen, boatswain's mate third class, and Wayne F. Martin, radioman third class, who were also aboard the *Skylark* that morning, remembered a slightly different version of the final messages from the *Thresher*. Mowen remembered having heard the submarine report "experiencing minor difficulty." They too were sure of the sounds of air being blown under pressure.

The statements of these men and the log of the *Skylark,* which was read at the session, indicated that something was definitely wrong inside the *Thresher* before the *Skylark* lost contact with her. But the rest of the Navy had known nothing of those last messages and sounds until the afternoon session of the inquiry on April 13—almost three and a half days after the *Thresher* was lost. Admiral Anderson had told a press conference held 25 hours after the *Thresher* was lost that the last messages from the submarine indicated everything was proceeding normally. The Chief of Navy Information said the Navy in Washington "absolutely did not know of the sounds" until Lieutenant Watson's testimony was heard at Portsmouth.

More witnesses were heard on the 13th. Joseph Shafer, an older brother of two chief petty officers who were lost in the *Thresher,* volunteered to appear before the court and was heard. Shafer himself was a retired Navy chief petty officer. He testified that both of his brothers were most enthusiastic about the Navy in general and the *Thresher* in particular. But Shafer stated that his brothers were "not sure" that people who worked on the *Thresher* during her overhaul had done their job. He said there was a jocular attitude of "what's going to be wrong this time" on the part of his late brothers. David Main, a welder at the Electric Boat yard and a brother-in-law of the Shafers, substantiated the testimony of Joseph Shafer regarding his brothers.

Captain Donald Kern, head of the Submarine Branch of the Bureau of Ships, was the next witness. He testified that at 8,400 feet the *Thresher's* hull would rupture and flood, her compartments completely destroyed. Some debris would float to the surface, he noted.

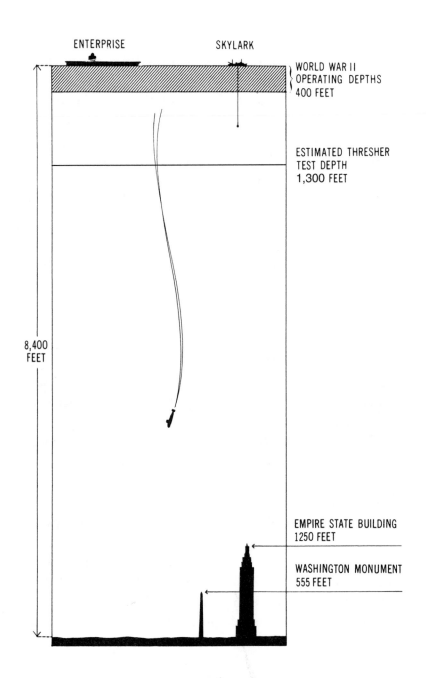

ENTERPRISE

SKYLARK

WORLD WAR II
OPERATING DEPTHS
400 FEET

ESTIMATED THRESHER
TEST DEPTH
1,300 FEET

8,400
FEET

EMPIRE STATE BUILDING
1250 FEET

WASHINGTON MONUMENT
555 FEET

The following witness, Navy Lieutenant Jack Sousae, presented the court with the debris that had been recovered at the *Thresher* search scene. Then chemists and radiation experts from the Portsmouth yard discussed the material. No abnormal radioactivity was found on the debris, which matched materials in the *Thresher*.

The Saturday session was long. Admiral Austin finally adjourned the court at 6:11 p.m.

Lieutenant Commander Stanley Hecker, commanding officer of the rescue ship *Skylark*, led the parade of witnesses when the court again came to order at Portsmouth on Monday, April 15. The *Skylark*'s skipper corroborated the log and the basic testimony given Saturday by others from the ship, although he too differed on the exact wording of the *Thresher*'s last messages. He recalled the last message as: "Experiencing minor problem. . . . Have positive angle. . . . Attempting to blow." He described the voice from the *Thresher* as "very relaxed."

Commander Hecker said that shortly after this communication with the *Thresher* he distinctly heard the sounds of air being blown into the submarine's tanks to displace water and give the craft more buoyancy. Then he heard what appeared to be a voice trying to break through the noise of the blowing air, but he could not understand the words.

And what of the sound Lieutenant Watson described as "a ship breaking up—like a compartment collapsing"? Commander Hecker said he could not recall the sound and was unfamiliar with it anyway. The 36-year-old commanding officer told the court he had no information on the *Thresher*'s capabilities and that the underwater telephone was the only electronic equipment in the *Skylark* that matched the *Thresher*'s equipment.

In a voice that suggested great concern, he told Admiral Austin: "I was willing to put down my four anchors, or even six anchors, every piece of line aboard, all my buoys or anything else to mark the spot, but I had only 7,200 feet of nylon line." Thus the *Skylark* was unable to even mark the grave of the *Thresher* after she lost communications with the submarine.

The court particularly questioned Commander Hecker about the last messages from the *Thresher*. He was also questioned closely about an unidentified ship sighted during a search of the area near where the *Thresher* went down.

Commander Hecker described the vessel as "of a dirty color, possibly gray once." The *Skylark* moved to within 6,000 yards of the ship, which "seemed to be lying to." But he said he could not remember where she went after he had determined that the ship was not the *Thresher*. When first sighted, the ship was thought to be the sail of a submarine, said Hecker. And, "being anxious, we possibly hoped it was," he added.

After hearing Commander Hecker's testimony the court recessed for a memorial service for the men lost in the *Thresher*. As the room emptied the inquiry seemed to be uncovering more mysteries than it was solving. Why had Commander Hecker waited more than an hour and a half before signaling that he had lost communications with the *Thresher?* Why had he not told that the submarine's final messages indicated some difficulties? What of the allegation that the people who worked on the *Thresher* during her overhaul were not doing their job? And, did the unidentified ship sighted in the search area have any relation to the *Thresher's* disappearance?

On the afternoon of the 15th the court heard from Commander Howard Larcombe, commanding officer of the diesel-electric submarine *Dogfish* and the senior submarine commander at Portsmouth. He told the court that Lieutenant Commander Harvey had assured him the day before

Above: The 15-foot-diameter sphere of the AN/BQQ-2 sonar dome prior to installation. The sphere was fitted with 1,241 hydrophones. *Below:* The *Thresher,* launched bow first, takes to the water for the first time. Her stern, shown here, had not yet been fitted with a propeller. The platform on the deck was a temporary structure installed for the launch.

Above: The *Thresher*'s interior, showing the bow sonar sphere, amidships torpedo tubes, and ot
and other machinery. *Below:* The *Thresher* cruises on the surface prior to commissioni

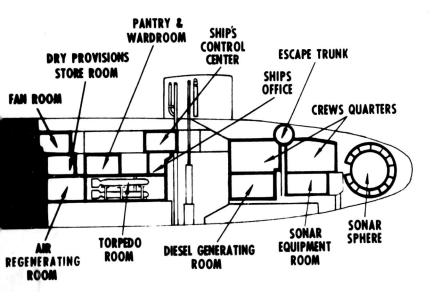

tails of the submarine's "front end." The "rear end" contained the ship's S5W reactor, turbines,
though she looked sleek, the *Thresher* was cantankerous and awkward on the surface.

Top: A bow-on view of the *Thresher* shows her circular hull, small sail structure, and large diving planes. *Above left:* Commander Dean L. Axene, first commanding officer of the *Thresher. Right:* Lieutenant Commander John W. Harvey, the second and last commanding officer.

Above: The submarine rescue ship *Skylark*, which escorted the *Thresher* on her last cruise. *Right:* Vice Admiral H.G. Rickover. *Below:* The control room of a *Thresher*-class submarine. The helmsman sits in the right-hand seat; the standby helmsman and planesman sits in the left-hand seat; the officer of the watch stands behind them; the chief of the watch is at far left, ready to operate the diving panel or ballast control board.

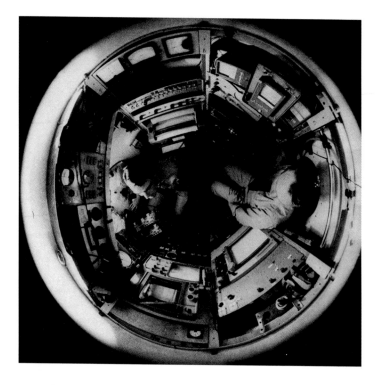

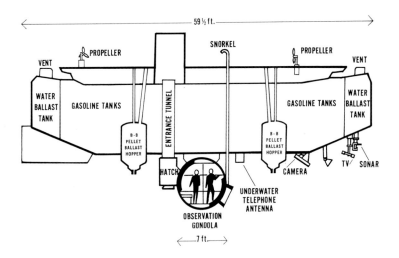

Above left: The cramped conditions inside the *Trieste*'s gondola. The inner diameter is 6½ feet — just enough to pack in three men plus a host of equipment and the controls needed to operate the craft. *Below left:* The discarded submarine *Toro,* with stripes to help visual identification when it was planned to sink her at the *Thresher* site. *Above:* Cross-section of the *Trieste. Below right:* Technicians work on the *Trieste* in Boston Harbor. Note the external electric motors and propellers. Lieutenant Commander Keach, wearing officer's cap, stands on deck.

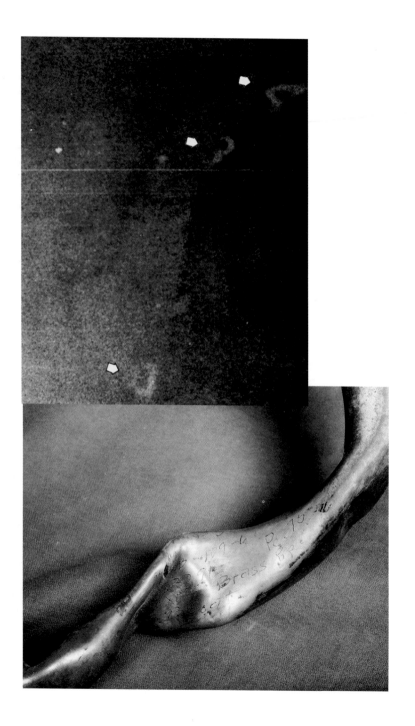

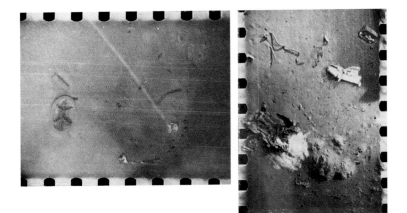

Left: The bow section of the *Thresher* as photographed on the ocean floor by the bathyscaph *Trieste* on August 24, 1963. Arrows point to draft mark numbers 4, 3, and 0 on the bow. (Draft mark numbers indicate how deep a submarine is lying when she is on the surface.) *Below left:* The pipe from the *Thresher* — imprinted with "593 boat" and job and serial numbers — was recovered by the *Trieste. Above left:* A watertight door from inside the *Thresher. Above right:* Rock wool insulation. *Below left:* This air bottle, similar to those in submarines, had not been crushed by water pressure because it was fully charged with air or was holed and filled with water. *Below right:* A piece of pipe, broken at both ends, lying on the ocean floor.

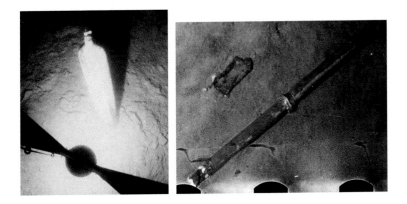

Top: The Board of Inquiry into the loss of the *Thresher*. From left are Captain James B. Osborn, Rear Admiral Lawrence R. Daspit, Vice Admiral Bernard L. Austin, Captain William C. Hushing, and Captain Norman C. Nash. *Above:* Three of nineteen packages of "O" rings recovered by drag lines from the *Conrad* on May 27, 1963. They were the first recovered items that were known definitely to have been aboard the *Thresher* when she was lost. *Bottom:* Oil samples, plastic debris, gloves, and tube of "baker's flavoring" recovered from the *Thresher* search area on the day the submarine was lost.

Above: Lieutenant Commander Donald Keach (*right*) with Secretary of the Navy, Fred Korth. *Below:* Overhead and side views of the original proposal for a Deep Submergence Rescue Vehicle (DSRV), designed after the loss of the *Thresher*. The vehicle could carry fourteen survivors.

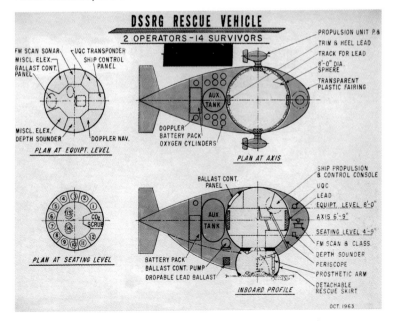

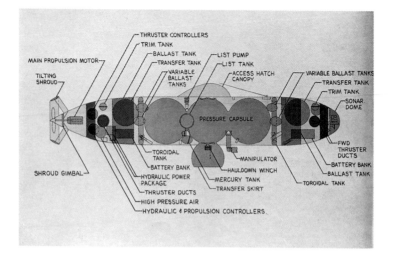

Above: Cutaway of the DSRV as built, showing the three interconnected pressure spheres; the first was the control sphere while the two after spheres hold 24 survivors plus a crewman. *Below:* Lockheed engineers insert the three-sphere pressure hull into the fiberglass hull. (Lockheed photo)

Above: The DSRV *Avalon* mated with a submarine; note the transfer skirt, which mates with the "mother" submarine's after hatch. *Below:* The DSRV *Avalon* mated to the nuclear-propelled submarine *Billfish* heading to sea on an exercise.

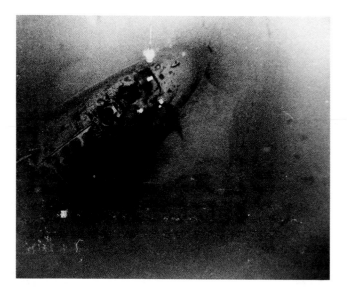

Above: The bow section of the USS *Scorpion* on the ocean floor, some 400 miles southwest of the Azores. *Top right:* The Soviet missile submarine *K-219* (NATO Yankee) on the surface east of Bermuda after suffering a missile explosion. *Right:* The Soviet nuclear submarine *K-8* (NATO November) sinking off the coast of Spain. *Bottom:* An Oscar-class Soviet cruise missile submarine similar to the *Kursk,* which sank in the Barents Sea.

Above: A Charlie II-class cruise missile submarine similar to the Soviet *K-429* — a nuclear submarine that sank twice. *Below:* The *Komsomolets* (NATO Mike) was probably the world's most advanced submarine when she plunged into the ocean depths in the Norwegian Sea. As the submarine sank, five men used her escape chamber to reach the surface, but poisonous fumes killed four.
(Norwegian Air Force)

he took the *Thresher* to sea that his ship and crew were ready for the trials. Commander James Bellah, a staff officer from Submarine Development Group 2, confirmed that Harvey was "ready to go."

One of the Navy's leading engineering officers, Captain William Heronemus, testified next. As the repair and ship-building superintendent of the Portsmouth yard, he was intimately familiar with the work that had been done on the *Thresher* during the past nine months. "I have known no other ship in a higher state of readiness for sea than the *Thresher*," he declared. Captain Heronemus, discussing the personnel on board the *Thresher* on her last cruise, described them as competent. Another top shipyard officer, Captain William Roseborough, the yard's planning officer, also testified.

The day's final witness was Vice Admiral Elton W. Grenfell, commander of the Atlantic Fleet Submarine Force. Grenfell—like Captain Roseborough before him—said that no pressure had been put on the shipyard or the commanding officer of the *Thresher* to accelerate her return to operational status. Commenting on the duration of the overhaul, he noted that "delays in shipyards are common and understandable on new type ships." Admiral Grenfell also stated that the experience level of the crew was as good as that aboard any nuclear submarine in the fleet.

While Admiral Grenfell was technically correct, in reality there was a rush by all concerned to have the *Thresher* return to sea. The Navy wanted to determine as soon as possible the effectiveness of the *Thresher* and her sister ships, two of which, the *Permit* and *Plunger*, were in commission when the *Thresher* was lost. With Soviet nuclear submarine construction accelerating, U.S. attack submarine construction was slowing as priority was being given to the Polaris program.

When Admiral Grenfell was asked by the court if he had a personal theory of what happened to the *Thresher,* he replied that his theory was classified. The court room was then cleared for 25 minutes while he made his statement.

The only witness before the court of inquiry on April 16 was Rear Admiral Lawson P. Ramage, Grenfell's deputy. He testified that although he had commanded the search for the *Thresher,* he was unaware for two days that the submarine's last clear message was one indicating possible difficulties. Admiral Ramage said he did not learn of the Wednesday morning message from the *Thresher* until Lieutenant Watson, the *Skylark*'s navigator, boarded his ship on Friday for transfer to Portsmouth to testify before the court of inquiry.

Admiral Ramage told the court: "I have come to the conclusion that this additional information would not have changed our search plans at the site." However, he added: "An initial evaluation would have been made sooner." Ramage also said that the strange ship sighted in the search area was identified as the Norwegian fishing trawler *Juviel.* He said the fishermen were passing nearby and, in his opinion, had no significance in the loss of the *Thresher.*

Then Admiral Ramage described the oil slicks and debris, such as bits of cork and plastic and work gloves, found over a 20-mile radius during the two days after the *Thresher* was lost. He confirmed Admiral Grenfell's remarks of the previous day concerning the experience level of the *Thresher*'s crew.

After hearing Admiral Ramage's testimony, Admiral Austin recessed the court explaining "the court has reached a point in its deliberations beyond which it cannot continue without the presence of a person not now in Portsmouth. The court will reconvene as soon as possible. . . ."

That person was Lieutenant Commander Hecker, the commanding officer of the *Skylark*. That same day Commander Hecker returned to Portsmouth from New London, where his ship was docked. Upon his appearance in the courtroom, Hecker was cited for his failure to report the last messages from the *Thresher* "for an unreasonable length of time."

Admiral Austin told Hecker: "The court has concluded that your conduct as commanding officer, USS *Skylark,* as revealed by evidence presented to the court, appears to be subject to inquiry. The evidence in question reflects that you failed fully to inform higher authority of all the information available to you pertinent to the circumstances attending the last transmissions received by *Skylark* from *Thresher* on 10 April 1963, as it was your duty to do, for an unreasonable length of time. The court wishes to emphasize at this time that this apparent failure on your part cannot conceivably have contributed in any way to the loss of the USS *Thresher* and those on board. You are accordingly designated as a party before this court. Counsel for the court will now inform you of your rights as such."

Captain Saul Katz, counsel for the court, informed Commander Hecker that he had the right to obtain his own counsel, examine records of all evidence thus far given, cross-examine witnesses, introduce witnesses, and present a closing argument at the conclusion of the inquiry.

Commander Hecker said that he would exercise his right to obtain counsel and examine previous testimony. The court then recessed to allow him time to get counsel. For his lawyer, Hecker obtained the services of Louis P. Gray, a retired Navy captain, a former submariner, and former shipmate of Hecker's. Gray had been a Pentagon legal expert and military adviser to presidential candidate Richard M. Nixon.

Although the court of inquiry was not trying the *Skylark's* skipper, for all intents and purposes Lieutenant Commander Hecker's naval career was now at stake.

A second "party" to the inquiry was named at his own request when the court convened again on April 18. Rear Admiral Charles A. Palmer, commander of the Portsmouth Naval Shipyard, asked and received permission to be made "an interested party" since the *Thresher* was built and overhauled in his yard. This would provide him the right to be represented by counsel, to be present at all sessions, and to question witnesses.

Next the court heard from the men most acquainted with the *Thresher* before she was lost—crewmen who stayed ashore the morning of April 9. Lieutenant Raymond McCoole, the submarine's electrical officer, had not been aboard because of his wife's eye injury, and Frank DeStefano, chief machinist's mate, was being transferred to nuclear power training. Both told of problems aboard the *Thresher*.

They testified that there had been trouble with the main sea water valve in the *Thresher* during the nine months the submarine was undergoing overhaul. This was a large valve that admitted water for several of the submarine's cooling systems.

Lieutenant McCoole also said that the air systems of the *Thresher* had been a continuing problem; that there had been errors in the indicators that showed whether or not the submarine was on an even keel; that 20 per cent of the hydraulic system's valves had been installed backwards; that the periscope mechanisms were found to have been installed backwards; and that the diving plane and rudder mechanisms had been found defective and were replaced the day before the *Thresher* went to sea. He told the court that in March the *Thresher* began a "fast cruise" that was halted by Lieutenant

Commander Harvey after two days because of difficulties in the submarine's air system. (The fast cruise—made with the submarine "fast" to a dock—was later successfully completed before the *Thresher* went to sea.)

"The air systems were a continuing problem as I recollect," Lieutenant McCoole testified. "The reducers in the air system were not functioning properly. They were replaced numerous times. I don't recall how many. It would seem that every time the work day ended a reducer was replaced."

These air systems were of vital importance to the *Thresher.* They blew air into the submarine's ballast tanks, forcing out water and providing the buoyancy necessary for coming to the surface.

He noted that on the night of April 8—the night before the *Thresher* went to sea—shipyard workers were correcting the submarine's sail and stern diving planes. These small, wing-like structures were the primary means of controlling the submarine's depth when she was underway.

After enumerating the ills of the *Thresher* during her nine-month overhaul, Lieutenant McCoole explained that all mechanical faults that had been discovered had been corrected.

Chief DeStefano, who was transferred from the *Thresher* the day before she left on her last cruise, said that the flooding drills held during the aborted March "fast cruise" were not as successful as they should have been because the crew was not familiar with a design change in the position of the submarine's sea valves. He said that during the drills certain vital check valves with tricky labeling were found to have been installed backwards. This mistake, he said, was caught by the submarine's crew and corrected.

Both Lieutenant McCoole and Chief DeStefano were lavish in their praise of Commander Dean Axene, the *Thresher*'s first commanding officer, and of Lieutenant Commander Harvey, who went down with the submarine.

The parade of witnesses continued. Most of the sessions were now held behind closed doors, for the court was hearing testimony on the *Thresher*'s design and construction—information of great value to other nations.

Frederick L. Downs, a chemist at the Portsmouth shipyard, introduced a piece of charred plastic shielding for a nuclear reactor, which had been found floating near where the *Thresher* was lost. He said the 18-inch-square fragment showed signs of having been hit by a "rush of flame." There was no evidence of a prolonged fire, he testified. The yellow-colored plastic was of the type used in reactor shielding of *Thresher*-class submarines, but there was no identification on the debris to definitely link it to the *Thresher*. Downs said he was continuing a series of tests to determine what caused a "jagged fracture" of the shield. So far tests for tearing effects, impact, and compression had failed to explain the jagged edges.

Other debris introduced to the court included two large pieces of padding from a life jacket like those carried in nuclear-propelled submarines, and several pieces of white and yellow plastic also found in nuclear subs. Downs noted that some of the smaller pieces of plastic were also charred and, like the larger piece, had jagged or torn edges.

Another shipyard chemist, John E. Carrigan, said the larger piece of plastic had several fragments of metal imbedded in it. He described the metal pieces as ranging in size from the head of a common pin to a split pea. Some of the metal was analyzed as lead and some as a low-alloy steel, he said.

"Every item could have come from the *Thresher*," he testified.

Another witness who knew the *Thresher* well was Lieutenant Commander William J. Cowhill, executive officer of the submarine from March 1962, to January 1963. He rated the *Thresher*'s construction and overhaul work at the Portsmouth yard as excellent—"with one reservation, the silver brazing process on piping."

Silver brazing is the process of welding metals on submarines with silver solder instead of the more common lead solder. The silver solder melts at a higher temperature than lead and gives a much stronger joint. There were hundreds of silver brazed joints in the maze of pipes in the *Thresher*, many of them on pipes that penetrated the craft's pressure hull.

Asked by the court to elaborate on his testimony regarding the silver brazing, Commander Cowhill said: "Up to the degree we had reached in this art, the Portsmouth Naval Shipyard is equal or better than other submarine builders, but we have reached only so far in this art."

The submarine's hydraulic system was "reliable as far as these systems on subs go," he said. "But I would like to see it better. It has always been a problem on submarines." However, he added that it did not pose a safety problem.

Commander Cowhill was asked to assess the air system in the *Thresher*. He replied: "There are limitations on blowing at depths. If we didn't have valve problems we wouldn't need a crew."

During the session, Captain Louis Gray, Lieutenant Commander Hecker's counsel, questioned Commander Cowhill about the final messages received from the *Thresher*. In reply, the former *Thresher* exec said that any one of four members of the *Thresher*'s crew, including Lieutenant Commander Harvey, could have been speaking into the UQC underwater telephone to the *Skylark*. (Commander Axene later told the author that he believed the *Thresher*'s telephone link to the *Skylark* would have been manned by any one of three persons in the ill-fated submarine—Lieutenant Commander Harvey, Lieutenant Commander Garner, the executive officer, or Aaron Gunter, quartermaster first class.)

The *Thresher*'s final messages "Experiencing minor problem. . . . Have positive angle. . . . Attempting to blow," were delivered in a calm voice, according to earlier testimony. Commander Cowhill said that from the previous testimony given it was his impression that the *Thresher* crew was not "really concerned" with the situation at that moment.

Commander Cowhill also noted that the *Thresher*'s crew had been proficient in all emergency techniques including those to combat flooding. There was "no better crew" in the service by the time the *Thresher* had finished her earlier trials before she began her overhaul at Portsmouth, he testified. Most of this crew was lost in the *Thresher*. (Cowhill soon would be ordered to command the *Thresher*'s sistership *Dace*.)

As the hearings of April 20 drew to a close the court prepared to take a day's leave for the following Sunday. But before the Saturday afternoon session ended, Vice Admiral Austin, the senior member of the court, politely told Rear Admiral Palmer, the shipyard commander, and Commander Shelley E. Rule, quality assurance superintendent at the yard, that "searching questions" would be asked in the next week's sessions.

"Well, Admiral Palmer," Admiral Austin said, "the court is conscious of the fact that the loss of the *Thresher* and those on board has been a particular source of not only sorrow but concern to this establishment which you head. The court appreciates the very high order of cooperation which it has been receiving from your organization despite the other duties imposed upon you, and I'm sure that you appreciate that this court, in view of the fact that your organization did perform the last work on the *Thresher* before it was lost, will have to ask very searching questions.

"I want you to understand that this is not done in any spirit of pointing any finger at anyone, but we must determine every fact we can in this case. And so, when our questions are very searching, I want you to understand that we are not being unkind. We are just doing our job, as I'm sure you appreciate we must do."

To Commander Rule, Admiral Austin added: "It seems that no degree of quality inspection would eliminate hazards in submarines if there is not absolute assurance that no valves were in wrong and no joints not properly inspected."

The parade of witnesses that began Monday morning, April 22, consisted in the main of Portsmouth engineers with blueprints in hand. Leading those to testify was Sherman Pelton, head of the quality assurance and analysis division. For an hour and a half he was questioned about the process of brazing and welding pipe joints in deep-diving submarines. He concluded his answers with the opinion that it was "very improbable" that any joint fitted in the *Thresher* during her overhaul would fail in a deep test dive. But Pelton had no explanation for the earlier testimony that the sea water valve system of the *Thresher* had been installed backwards during the submarine's overhaul.

A supervising inspector, Robert E. Fite, said he thought "a lot better work could be done" in installing flexible hose connections in submarines like the *Thresher*. However, he said that the probability of a failure of the flexible hoses in the *Thresher* was "very, very remote, considering the extra-strength test they get."

Gerald W. French, assistant to the chief marine mechanical engineer at Portsmouth, said that the *Thresher* had the best inspection process ever employed on flexible connections in any yard in the country.

William G. Poor, a group master in the production department, said that some flexible hoses had not been installed in the *Thresher* because of lack of time toward the end of the submarine's overhaul. However, he added that the *Thresher's* crew made a thorough inspection of all phases of the overhaul before going to sea and had pronounced the submarine ready. Benjamin Bragdon Jr., a naval architect, also testified.

The final witness of the day was Raymond Mattson, a torpedoman's mate first class assigned to the *Thresher.* He had been excused from the submarine's final voyage because he was on leave prior to being transferred to a shore station because of a nervous condition. Mattson listed what he called "deficiencies" of the *Thresher* when she put into Portsmouth for overhaul, but he said all had been corrected.

There was no session on the 23rd, as members of the court reviewed the record of the hearings to date and planned the future direction of the inquiry. To the south, at New London, the Polaris submarine *Lafayette* ran up her commission pennant and joined the Fleet. Although she was of a different underwater species than the *Thresher,* designed to fire long-range missiles into an enemy heartland rather than seek out and destroy other submarines, the *Lafayette* was still a close kin to the *Thresher.* The newer submarine incorporated many of the *Thresher's* design features and equipment. The *Lafayette* was also the lead ship for a class 31 Polaris submarines, and her commissioning seemed to emphasize the need for finding what had killed the *Thresher.*

On April 24, the court heard James C. Rogers, an assistant quality assurance division superintendent, say that "failure of a piping system would be the most hazardous condition that might occur" in a submarine. He said "many, many things" could have triggered the *Thresher* disaster, but failure of the piping "seems most likely."

The variety of intensive tests made on the *Thresher*'s hull and piping before she left the yard were also described by Rogers. He asserted that all but ten or twelve tests had been conducted on the *Thresher* prior to her sailing. The remaining tests were either minor ones or ones to be conducted at sea. He emphasized "nothing on the list would preclude the ship from going to sea. Safety was not involved."

Periodically on the 24th, 25th, 26th, and 27th the court went behind closed doors to hear secret testimony regarding the design, construction, and overhaul of the *Thresher*. A Marine sentry barred access to the chamber to all but those authorized by the court.

Cicero A. Lewis, a design engineer, testified behind the closed doors for 35 minutes. Then newsmen were admitted to the chamber briefly to hear him say the debris found floating in the Atlantic "could have" come from the *Thresher*.

Also heard in closed session was Frank Durham, who had been the senior shipyard representative during the *Thresher*'s shock tests off Key West a year earlier. Although his testimony was not disclosed, a Navy spokesman said the shock tests had "no connection with the *Thresher*'s casualty."

The "rush of flame" theory in the *Thresher* sinking was dismissed on April 26 with the testimony of Captain John J. Hinchy, who had supervised installation of the *Thresher*'s nuclear reactor. He told the court that he had conducted extensive tests on the block of yellow plastic recovered in the *Thresher* search area and determined that it had been blackened by "heavy concentrations of graphite or carbon." The discoloration, he explained, apparently came from the lubricant used in a machine that drilled two holes in the material to allow the plastic to fit around piping. Captain Hinchy said he was convinced no "rush of flame" caused the burn-like damage to the plastic, as theorized earlier in the hearings.

More of the men who had designed the *Thresher* and supervised her construction and overhaul were heard as the court continued, mostly in closed session.

A smallish man, clad in civilian clothes, hurried into the court of inquiry on Monday, the 29th. He was Vice Admiral H.G. Rickover, controversial head of the Navy's nuclear propulsion program. Before reading into the record two statements that he had issued on the two days following the disaster, Rickover said he would "like to say something about the crew."

He continued, "I and members of my group knew many of the crew members personally and were responsible for their selection, training, and encouragement. We knew their problems. Everyone knows how I felt about the crew. It was a personal loss to me. We can only hope that in giving their lives to their country they contributed to our future safety."

Admiral Rickover then said the reactor used in submarines and surface ships of the Navy was designed to minimize nuclear hazards. He declared that it was "physically impossible for the reactor to explode like a bomb." In addition, the design provided for protection against corrosion by sea water. "In event of a serious accident," he explained, "fuel elements will remain intact and none would be released." Danger, he said, could arise only "if the fuel elements were to melt or the boundary [shielding] were to rupture." But, he added, "There is no reason to believe any radiological problems were caused by loss of the *Thresher*."

Admiral Rickover also told the court that samples of the ocean bottom taken at the last known site of the *Thresher* showed the bottom to be free of radioactivity.

After 12 minutes of testimony in open session the room was cleared and Admiral Rickover discussed classified aspects of the *Thresher* and her loss behind closed doors for 90 minutes. When he left he refused to answer questions from newsmen.

More witnesses were heard in open and closed sessions. Then, on May 1, Admiral Austin announced that tests would be held to determine what a sudden rush of sea water would do to submarine equipment. The next day, the members of the court, clad in yellow rain slickers and gray shipyard helmets, looked on as a mockup of a submarine control panel was subjected to jets of water in a Portsmouth drydock. The force of the water in the tests would be similar to a stream of water entering a submarine operating at great depths.

The first blast of water lasted only three and a half seconds. It dented the control panel. A thin wisp of smoke spiraled up.

Next a seven-second stream of water smashed into the panel.

The damage was examined and discussed with the submarine-shipyard authorities on hand. Back in the courtroom the sessions were continued, mostly behind closed doors.

On May 7—almost a month after the *Thresher* was lost—the question of valves being installed backwards in the submarine was cleared up. Captain John D. Guerry, production officer of the Portsmouth yard, told a news conference that none of the valves was installed backwards. His statement was designed to clarify earlier testimony indicating some of the valves in the submarine were improperly installed. "There are 5,000 opportunities to put a valve in backwards. . . . But following exhaustive tests none was backwards when the ship sailed," Guerry stated.

He said valves were sometimes deliberately installed in reverse for certain tests, generally at dockside. But, by the time the *Thresher* put to sea, all valves were checked out and found to be in proper working order, he said. Captain Guerry also noted that there was "room for improvement" in the time taken to overhaul the *Thresher* before her final voyage.

The Chief of the Bureau of Ships—the Navy technical bureau charged with ship design, construction, repair, and overhaul—testified on May 9. Rear Admiral William A. Brockett, newly appointed head of the bureau, said that there were "obvious lessons to be learned" from the *Thresher*'s loss although he did not elaborate. He stated his belief that the *Thresher* design was basically sound and added: "The United States has the finest submarines in the world that can do things no one else can do."

His predecessor as chief of the bureau, Rear Admiral Ralph K. James, was the next witness. Admiral James said that at the request of the Secretary of the Navy he had gathered together an eight-man board of experts, some of whom were recalled from retirement, to examine every component of the *Thresher* design. Retired Rear Admiral A.I. McKee, one of the world's foremost submarine constructors, was named to head the special board.

Admiral James declared the *Thresher* "represented a significant step forward for ship silencing and depth to which submarines could go. We have had three analyses and reviews of the *Thresher*'s design, including one since she was lost. . . . [The] *Thresher* represented the finest in capability at sea and possessed the greatest of safety capabilities." He also said construction of submarines of the *Thresher* design would continue.

On May 13, testimony was again heard from personnel of the rescue ship *Skylark*. Lieutenant Commander Hecker, her commanding officer, said he had not felt that anything had happened to the *Thresher* until an oil slick appeared nine hours after the submarine's deep dive.

Then Hecker's attorney asked that the court withdraw the *Skylark*'s skipper as a party to the inquiry. Captain Gray told the court that while Hecker "doesn't for one minute hold that the court has branded him as scapegoat," a "substantial" segment of the public did hold that opinion.

After 41 minutes of deliberation in closed session it was announced that "the court has considered the testimony to date bearing on the loss of the USS *Thresher* and has received the motion and statement of Lieutenant Commander Hecker's counsel. The court, after such consideration, agrees that it no longer appears that Lieutenant Commander Hecker is involved in a material degree in the matter under investigation. Lieutenant Commander Hecker's designation as a party is accordingly withdrawn pursuant to his request."

During the next few days some witnesses were recalled, testimony from officers involved in the search for the *Thresher* was heard, and testimony was restudied. The court announced on May 16 that no further open hearings were expected. However, there was one more open session on June 1 at which the last witnesses were heard.

Almost two months after the hearings began, on Thursday, June 6, the court of inquiry announced that it had completed its work with the signing of the record of the proceedings of the investigation. The court recorded 1,700 pages of testimony and gathered some 255 charts, drawings, letters, photographs, directives, and other exhibits bearing on the loss of the *Thresher.* The words of 120 witnesses were included in the report.

Fifteen copies of the report were delivered the next day by Admiral Austin to Admiral H. Page Smith, Commander-in-Chief of the Atlantic Fleet, at Norfolk. Admiral Smith, who had overall supervision of all fleet activities and operations in the Atlantic, commented on and forwarded the report to

Washington. There it was studied by a host of Navy leaders and specialists. No word of the report was revealed to the public until noon on June 20, 1963. At exactly 12 o'clock Navy information officers began passing out copies of a three-page news release to waiting newsmen in the Department of Defense Public Affairs office. (For the complete release, see pages 182–184).

The first two paragraphs of the release presented the official Navy opinion of what killed the *Thresher*:

A flooding casualty in the engine room is believed to be the "most probable" cause of the sinking of the nuclear submarine USS THRESHER, lost April 10, 1963, 220 miles east of Cape Cod with 129 persons aboard.

The Navy believes it most likely that a piping system failure had occurred in one of the *THRESHER*'s salt water systems, probably in the engine room. The enormous pressure of sea water surrounding the submarine subjected her interior to a violent spray of water and progressive flooding. In all probability water affected electrical circuits and caused loss of power. THRESHER slowed and began to sink. Within moments she had exceeded her collapse depth and totally flooded. She came to rest on the ocean floor, 8,400 feet beneath the surface.

The news release went on to recount the known events of April 9–10 and tell of the work of the court of inquiry. Midway in the brief release was perhaps the most significant statement:

The record states that it is impossible, with the information now available, to obtain a more precise determination of what actually happened.

CHAPTER 9

A SEQUENCE OF EVENTS

There were those who knew what happened to the *Thresher*. Five, perhaps ten, maybe a score of men, and just possibly as many as 129. All were dead. Thus the theories of what killed the *Thresher* initially ran the gauntlet of possibility from enemy action to human error to the failure of a piping system.

It is known that at 7:47 a.m. on April 10 the *Thresher* was operating close to the surface when she rendezvoused with the rescue ship *Skylark* some 220 nautical miles east of Cape Cod. The day before the *Thresher* had conducted her shallow dives. At first she had gone down to about 60 feet (depth of keel), close enough to the surface to allow her to keep her extended radar mast exposed for contact with the *Skylark*. That first dive was made in about 185 feet of water. As the *Thresher* continued her shallow diving trials, she headed east and into deeper waters. It is believed she went down to about 400 feet in the course of the dives on April 9. The *Thresher* also made a full-power run at that time. The tests were acceptable to Lieutenant Commander Harvey, and he advised the *Skylark* that he was going ahead with the planned dive to the *Thresher*'s maximum operating or "test" depth on the morning of the

10th. About 12 hours were to be devoted to the deep dives. If all went well the *Thresher* would be tied up safe and sound at Portsmouth about 4 p.m. on April 11.

The transit from the shallow dive area to the meeting with the *Skylark* on the morning of the 10th was probably made at about 200 feet. According to the Navy, "she was probably at such depth as to avoid shipping, with occasional periscope depth. There was no set depth [for such a transit by nuclear submarines]." Since Commander Harvey had already made a careful shallow test dive on April 9, he had no hesitation about diving the *Thresher* rapidly to 400 feet on the morning of April 10. The remainder of the deep dive would be cautious, and all instruments would be scrutinized as the submarine slowly went deeper and deeper.

At 7:54 a.m. on the 10th the *Thresher* reached 400 feet and advised the *Skylark* that future references to depth would be made in terms of test depth—1,300 feet. There was always the possibility that a Soviet surface ship or even submarine could be in the area and able to intercept the relatively primitive UQC underwater telephone. Outside of a small circle of Navy officials and civilian engineers, and a large, but closed-mouth, group of submariners, the *Thresher*'s test depth was top secret at that time.

The *Thresher* slowly went deeper. Beyond the 400-foot mark the *Thresher* descended by small increments, probably 100 feet at a time. She reported being at one-half test depth at 8:09 a.m. Thus it can be assumed that at 8:09 the *Thresher* was at about 650 feet.

At 8:35, the *Thresher* reported her depth at "minus 300 feet" or roughly 1,000 feet. Carefully the *Thresher*'s crew checked the submarine's watertight integrity and conducted various tests, in part similar to those of the shallow dive the day before.

At 8:53, the *Thresher* reported she was proceeding to test depth. The *Thresher* had probably remained at "minus 300 feet" for 18 minutes, checking equipment and conducting tests, or perhaps she had gone slightly deeper during that time without actually reporting the change of depth to the *Skylark*. Possibly the *Thresher* went down another 100 feet in this period.

At 9:02 and again at 9:12, routine communications took place between the *Thresher* and the *Skylark*. Reviewing the previous estimates of depth, it appears that the *Thresher* would have descended another 100 feet by the time of the 9:02 or 9:12 message if she were going down 100 feet at a time:

ESTIMATED TIME	TIME INTERVAL	DEPTH
7:54		400 feet
8:09	15 minutes	650 feet
8:35	24 minutes	1,000 feet
8:53	18 minutes	1,000–1,100 feet
9:12	19 minutes	1,100–1,200 feet

These estimates must be assumed to be the maximum depths reached by the *Thresher* during the time periods indicated, for it is entirely possible that she remained at the same depth during a time interval to conduct tests. Although there is also a slight possibility that the *Thresher* did reach her test depth by the time of the 9:12 message, it seems unlikely. If the *Thresher* had been at her test depth she would have reported it at the 9:12 communications check.

Rather it appears that at 9:12 on the morning of April 10 the *Thresher* was approaching her test depth in what was so far a normal, safe, and seemingly routine test dive. According to Lieutenant Commander Hecker of the *Skylark*, about a minute later the *Thresher* made a report that indicated she was no longer conducting a normal or safe or routine operation. Approximately 9:13 was the beginning of the end of the *Thresher*.

The communication alluded to by those aboard the *Skylark* who were listening to the messages from the *Thresher* is somewhat uncertain. There were three parts to this message as reported: "experiencing minor problem," an allusion to "angle," and "attempting to blow."

"Experiencing minor problem." What is a minor problem in a complex nuclear-propelled submarine? For example, at 1,000 feet flooding through a six-inch pipe certainly would not be cause for a report of a minor problem. At a depth of 1,000 feet approximately 100,000 pounds of sea water would flood through a six-inch pipe in just one minute! Even flooding through a half-inch pipe would hardly be considered minor, due to the noise it would cause, the powerful spray that would cause confusion and make finding the pipe difficult, and the uncertainty as to what was happening.

Loss of control of the diving planes—provided that they were not jammed in such a way as to increase depth rapidly— might be considered minor. Even if the diving planes were jammed on "hard dive" the difficulty could still be classified as minor if the speed of the submarine through the water was not high.

The exact speed of the *Thresher* at 9:12 is not known. For positive control of the submarine, the commanding officer was probably conducting the test at a speed of five to ten knots, most likely nearer the higher speed.

Even loss of main propulsion power through an accidental reactor shutdown or other temporary failure in the main propulsion system might initially be considered minor, especially if the trim of the submarine had her on an even keel.

However, if the *Thresher* was steaming at ten knots, a loss of forward motion through the water would slowly cause a loss of buoyancy, unless the submarine was intentionally trimmed in a "positive" buoyant condition and was being "held down" by the affect of the craft's speed on her wing—like diving planes. As speed is reduced, a submarine normally and naturally acts "heavy" and "wants" to go deeper.

"Experiencing minor problem" indicates that no sudden catastrophic event befell the *Thresher*. Rather, this part of the message indicates that the initial event of a sequence took place about 9:13 a.m.

The second part of the message is less informative because it does not make sense to those familiar with submarines. Three versions of this second portion of the message were given: "have position angle," "have positive up angle," and "have position up angle."

A submariner speaks of "having an up angle" or a "down angle" to mean that the bow of the submarine is pointing up or down, respectively. The submariner pays exceedingly close attention to this angle, and instruments can measure it accurately to within one quarter to one half of a degree. A submariner does not use the term "position up angle" or "position down angle." "Have positive up angle" may have meant the bow of the submarine was pointing up and the submarine was attempting to head for the surface—if that was the wording of the message. The literal expression "have position angle" is entirely meaningless. The report of this phase of the *Thresher*'s message was undoubtedly in error. Communications via underwater sound telephone are at best very poor and not unlike a long-distance, short-wave radio transmission, which is "fuzzy." Further, the sound transmission leaving the *Thresher*, in addition to traveling directly up to the *Skylark*, also traveled to the rescue ship via a bounce off the ocean floor, causing a reverberation or echo sound at the receiver. Often approximate knowledge of the message to be received assists the receiving ship in interpreting the message.

In the event, little light can be shed on the *Thresher* mystery from the second portion of the message.

The third portion of the message, "attempting to blow up," could be revealing. "Blow up" to a submariner means forcing high pressure air into the ballast tanks to expel the main ballast water, thus lightening the submarine so that she will go up.

Lieutenant Commander Harvey apparently decided, whatever the trouble and however minor it was, to shed the *Thresher*'s main ballast in order to give her more buoyancy. Since the same amount or greater upward lift could also be provided by increasing speed coupled with proper use of his diving planes, it appears that he did not have the ability to control either propulsion, and hence speed, or the diving planes. For example, a simple mathematical computation shows that had the *Thresher* been able to make ten knots and obtain a 30-degree up-angle with her planes, with neutral buoyancy the submarine would have gone up at the rate of some 500 feet per minute. With complete control of speed and diving plane action the *Thresher* could—under normal circumstances—have come up to the surface even faster if necessary.

Probably this non-availability of propulsion or diving plane control was the minor difficulty the submarine announced seconds earlier.

Further, this portion of the message, as reported, did not say "am blowing up," but rather "attempting to blow up." This is disturbing because "attempting" implies the high-pressure air is not expelling water from the ballast tanks as desired or, if it is, that the submarine is still not getting the needed buoyancy. This is all the more disturbing because there is a minimum of moving parts between the high-pressure air in a submarine's storage flasks and the pipes leading this air into the main ballast tanks.

The report "attempting to blow up" has the same effect on a submariner as hearing the driver of an automobile say, "I am attempting to put on the brakes." The experienced driver knows that braking a car is a simple, almost instantaneous action. Hearing such a statement makes one imagine the brake is being applied with no noticeable effect on the car.

Was there some mishap with the high-pressure air system in the *Thresher*? According to Lieutenant Watson's testimony, he heard the message "attempting to blow up" and then, for a few seconds, he heard the sound of compressed air. Roy Mowen, boatswain's mate third class, recalled hearing the compressed air sounds in the background as the *Thresher* reported "attempting to blow." And, indeed, the sound of compressed air may even have been heard before the "attempting to blow" part of the message.

If the message was received first, it would mean that, after "attempting" to blow up, the *Thresher* was finally successful, and the sound of air under pressure meant the submarine had started to blow up.

Had the message and sound been received simultaneously, the garble of the message would be understandable since the sound of compressed air flowing would seriously interfere with the sound reception (not unlike the affect of lightning on radio reception).

The estimate of hearing air under pressure for "several seconds" is very significant. If the *Thresher* wanted to blow up from near test depth, she would probably blow until she was well on the way to the surface, much longer than just a few seconds. If the message was received after the *Thresher* had started blowing air, the "attempting" would make more sense. In this case, however, the men in the *Thresher* would have begun to be concerned for their safety. Something had happened which, although at the time considered to be minor, caused Commander Harvey to want to expel his main ballast. The *Thresher* tried, and she could not.

Without control of speed and diving planes together or without high-pressure air to expel ballast, the *Thresher* could be in serious trouble at any depth—even a few feet below the surface, depending upon the trim of the submarine.

A sequence of events takes form.

For four minutes—as the *Thresher* is "attempting to blow up"—there is no communication. Then, at 9:17, the *Thresher* transmits a message ending with "test depth." It has been generally supposed that "exceeding" was one of the words preceding "test depth."

During these four minutes there was definite suspicion aboard the *Skylark* that all was not normal in the *Thresher*. Lieutenant Commander Hecker, commanding officer of the *Skylark,* personally took the *Skylark's* microphone and asked repeatedly: "Are you in control?" It is possible that Commander Hecker's attempt to communicate with the *Thresher* via the UQC prevented the rescue ship from hearing messages coming the other way in much the same way communication is impaired when two people talk to each other at the same time during a telephone conversation.

The *Thresher*'s failure to communicate during the four minutes—if Commander Hecker's calls were not blanking out those of the *Thresher*—could be interpreted in one of three ways:

First, it is possible that the sequence of events had quickly progressed to the point where those in the *Thresher* realized that disaster was imminent and were too busy trying to save themselves to take time out to communicate with the *Skylark*, which could not render any assistance.

Second, there is the possibility that during those four minutes the situation was static, with the *Thresher* simply hovering at about test depth, perhaps even rising at a very slow rate, but that there was not yet serious concern in the *Thresher*. In those minutes the crew was possibly busy restoring propulsion or tracing down the trouble in the high pressure air system. In this case, communication would have been postponed for a few minutes until a definite report could be transmitted.

Third—and a very definite possibility—is that the *Thresher* had lost electrical power to some or all of her lighting and electrical equipment, including her underwater telephone. Lieutenant Watson testified that seconds after the 9:17 message that ended with "test depth" he heard "the sound of a ship breaking up . . . like a compartment collapsing."

While the reported timing of all messages after the 9:12 routine communication could easily be in error by as much as a minute and quite possibly more, the timing must be assumed to be correct. Thus, about five minutes had elapsed between the initial trouble in the *Thresher* and the "sound of a ship breaking up." As the *Thresher* lost her battle to return to the surface, she began to plummet to the ocean floor, down into the depths where the tremendous pressure would destroy her.

The U.S. Navy constructs submarines to withstand one and a half times the pressure of their designed test depth. The ratio of the "test depth" to "collapse depth" of a submarine is therefore nominally two-to-three. This is a safety factor. The collapse depth is based on both mathematical calculations and model tests. The latter are not always conclusive since hydrodynamic scaling factors are difficult to calculate accurately. It is safe to assume that the collapse depth of the *Thresher* was approximately 1,950 feet.

The sequence of casualties suffered by the *Thresher* apparently caused a fateful increase of some 600 feet—from test depth to collapse depth—in five agonizing minutes.

Regardless of what the *Thresher*'s "minor problem" was, as she neared collapse depth she had major problems—fittings and pipes began to give way, admitting powerful jets of water that pushed aside men struggling to plug them and shorted out electrical equipment, making corrective action impossible. The additional weight of water thus admitted to the *Thresher* drove her still deeper at an ever-increasing speed. The submarine's hull groaned under the increasing pressure that tried to crush in her air-filled interior.

There were probably no serious personnel casualties at this point. But all men inside the submarine now sensed that they were rushing toward disaster and groped frantically for some avenue of escape or survival. Suddenly, the insulating cork that lined the submarine's interior began to crack and possibly flake off. Pipes began pulling apart as the water pressure began to "pull" the submarine's hardened steel like taffy. An instant later the hull imploded.

In a fraction of a second millions of pounds of water under tremendous pressure smashed the submarine's hull, twisting portions of it, disintegrating other parts of it along with the lighter materials inside it. Death was instantaneous and painless to all 129 men within the submarine.

The theory that water filled the plummeting *Thresher* before she could implode is generally discounted because the additional weight of the water would accelerate the downward rate and cause an implosion before the hull could fill with water. As the *Thresher* imploded and was torn apart, there could have been no air pockets to keep her "afloat" in a limbo somewhere between her collapse depth and the ocean floor. Instead, the remains of the *Thresher* rained down on the ocean floor almost a mile and a half below.

But what was the "minor" difficulty the *Thresher* encountered at about 9:13 that led to the worst submarine disaster in history? Even though the event was "minor" the *Thresher*'s commanding officer soon began to blow his main ballast tanks. Thus it appears that the minor difficulty was probably one to cause the *Thresher* to become heavy. This would most probably occur as a result of losing propulsion or taking on water. Loss of propulsion might have been a result of the latter condition.

The Navy's Court of Inquiry concluded that the "most probable" cause of the *Thresher*'s loss, with the information available, was failure of a piping system. Again, it seems doubtful that any submariner would consider flooding at or near test depth, regardless of how slight, as a "minor" difficulty. It is always possible that the report from the scene of the flooding inside of the *Thresher* could somehow have been garbled on its way to the control room, where a misinterpretation may have occurred, resulting in the report of a minor problem.

More probable, it appears that the initial minor difficulty was the loss of propulsion. With the loss of forward motion the *Thresher* began to sink deeper and deeper as a result of her heavy water ballast, which it was decided to expel. However, before the downward motion of the submarine could be halted—and before she reached her collapse depth—the increasing water pressure began to rupture some of the numerous pipes penetrating the submarine's pressure hull. This water drove the submarine still deeper and she imploded.

Following the Court of Inquiry's "most probable" cause—that the initial difficulty was a piping system failure—the flooding casualty could have been through a small (one- or two-inch) pipe or a larger opening (possibly four to six inches). Several piping systems of these diameters penetrated the *Thresher*'s engineering spaces. Again, because serious flooding would not have been reported as a minor problem, the smaller sizes seem more probable. At approximately the *Thresher*'s test depth, water entering through a one- or two-inch pipe would be shooting forth like the water shot from a high-pressure fire hose of comparable diameter. The water—possibly hitting other pipes or equipment and turning into a powerful spray—might have struck and shorted out a switchboard, causing a loss of power. Or, the force of the water might have knocked over a key member of the engine room crew. He might have been thrown against a switchboard or other control panel or, in his efforts to keep from being pushed away by the water, he might have grabbed blindly for something to hang on to and grabbed a vital control switch. Any of these actions could have occurred and led to the impending disaster.

Flooding or loss of propulsion appear to be the most probable initial incident that caused the death of the *Thresher*. However, there are other "possible" causes. Some are rather remote, but nonetheless they are possible.

The Court of Inquiry, it was noted in the release of its findings, reported that "the evidence does not establish that the deaths of those embarked in *Thresher* were caused by the intent, fault, negligence or inefficiency of any person or persons in the naval service or connected therewith." While this statement has been looked upon as primarily absolving shipyard personnel in the disaster, it was also interpreted to mean that the *Thresher*'s loss was not caused by one of her crewmen running amuck. Submariners are given psychological examinations. Indications are that all who went out in the *Thresher*—including the civilians—were "sane" by accepted standards. Also, the term "minor problem" appears to indicate mechanical troubles and does not lend itself to describing a crazed sailor.

The possibility of an internal explosion must be ruled out primarily because the *Skylark* heard no such sound on her UQC underwater telephone. An explosion powerful enough to critically wound the *Thresher* would have been heard by the *Skylark*. Also, the *Thresher* had no torpedoes on board and Admiral Rickover stated that a bomb-like explosion of the *Thresher*'s nuclear reactor was impossible. His statements, plus lack of abnormal radioactivity measurements in the search area, help rule out the possibility of a nuclear explosion.

Immediately after the *Thresher* was lost the theory of sabotage reared its head. Four years before the *Thresher* entered the Portsmouth yard for her overhaul, the pioneer nuclear-powered submarine *Nautilus* steamed into the yard for a major overhaul. During her stay at Portsmouth, several attempts were made to sabotage the nuclear submarine. Two hundred and thirty-seven separate and deliberate cuts were found in armored cable-type electrical wiring in the submarine. Most of them had been made during a five- or six-day period. A large-scale investigation of the *Nautilus* sabotage by the Federal Bureau of Investigation failed to discover the saboteurs, even though FBI agents investigated the background of everyone connected with the overhaul. Although no arrests were made, the agents did encounter several disgruntled civilian workmen at the Portsmouth yard.

After the cable cuttings—officially labeled as "intentional damage"—during October of 1959, work continued without further reported incident until the following June. At that time a hose used to test the submarine's evaporators was cut. The Navy said later that a crew member was responsible, but refused to give any details.

Intentional damage was also reported aboard the nuclear-propelled submarine *Snook*. On December 21, 1959, while the *Snook* was in drydock at Pascagoula, Mississippi, it was discovered that someone had cut through the elbow of some piping in the submarine.

Less than a month after the *Snook* incident possible sabotage was discovered aboard the nuclear-propelled missile cruiser *Long Beach*. The then-unfinished *Long Beach* was at Quincy, Massachusetts, when it was discovered that a 3½-inch armored anti-mine cable had been cut in three places. Although termed "relatively insignificant," this incident was also carefully investigated by the FBI as well as by Naval Intelligence.

Sabotage is usually connected with a deliberate attempt by an enemy agent. However, because of the circumstances it is generally accepted that these incidents were a form of adult vandalism or mischievousness on the part of a civilian worker or possibly naval personnel. It appears the purpose of the sabotage was to delay the ships involved rather than to cause their loss. Possibly these sabotage efforts could be traced to a sailor who wanted to delay his ship's going back to sea, or a yard worker who, fearing for his job, wanted the ship to remain in the yard as long as possible. Perhaps, for similar reasons, the *Thresher* was "sabotaged." The damage might have been minor—a few nuts loosened or removed; not enough to sink the submarine, but enough to hold up her sailing if the damage was discovered.

Or, the *Thresher* may have been sabotaged by carelessness. When the nuclear-propelled submarine *Triton* began her historic around-the-world submerged cruise in early 1960, one of her ventilation valves would not close. Although there was a double valve in the ventilation system—"just in case"—the faulty valve was still described as "critically important" by Captain Edward L. Beach, the *Triton's* skipper. Investigation of the valve disclosed that a smashed, rusted flashlight was lodged in the valve seat. It probably had been left by a careless workman, according to Captain Beach.

Although the Navy officially called sabotage "a very remote possibility" in the loss of the *Thresher,* there are some submariners who believe that sabotage—either intentional or accidental—may well have killed the *Thresher.*

Akin to sabotage is poor workmanship. American industry and shipyards have often been the target of criticism for poor workmanship. Admiral Rickover has been one of the most vehement critics. Six months before the *Thresher* was lost he stated in a speech that "on more than one occasion I have been in a deeply submerged submarine when a failure occurred in a sea-water system because a fitting was of the wrong material. But for the prompt action of the crew, the consequences would have been disastrous. In fact I might not be here today."

Did a similar failure occur in the *Thresher?* Was the action of her crew not prompt enough? Hitting on faults in nuclear submarine construction, Admiral Rickover said: "Some of the types of difficulties we constantly encounter . . . have to do with faulty welding, faulty radiography and defective castings; that is, with deficiencies in basic conventional processes of present-day technology.

He continued, "The press frequently reports malfunctions of advanced components or systems caused by failure of a weld, improper use of a routine process, or use of defective

materials. Industry apparently considers such failures to be inevitable, since not enough is being done to correct the causes."
Going into more detail, Admiral Rickover explained:

Recently we discovered that a stainless steel fitting had been welded into a nickel-copper alloy piping system. The fitting had been certified by the manufacturer as nickel-copper, and had all the required certification data including chemistry and inspection results. In fact the words "nickel-copper" were actually etched in the fitting. Yet it was the wrong material! The system was intended for sea water service; had it been placed in operation with this stainless steel fitting a serious casualty would have resulted.

Not long ago we discovered a mix-up in the marking and packaging of welding electrodes which also could have had very unfortunate consequences. . . . During the next three months, while we were checking this matter in detail, we detected similar incorrect marking and packaging of electrodes in cans *from nearly every major electrode manufacturer in the United States.* [Admiral Rickover's emphasis]

Another quality control problem is caused by failure to follow specified procedures or drawings. Here is a case in point: Material which had required a special heat treatment was delivered for a shipboard application. On examining records, we found that the material had been processed at an incorrect temperature and had been in the furnace for an excessive length of time; also that the furnace temperature instruments had been out of calibration. The company concerned could not have done much worse.

Nuclear-powered submarines are complex structures!
(Six months after the *Thresher* was lost the Navy announced that all 31 nuclear-propelled submarines then under construction were being delayed. The Navy noted that "deficiencies in equipment and workmanship are contributing factors" to such delays.)

The theory has also been advanced that an underwater storm in the area where the *Thresher* went down caused her loss. Dr. Columbus Iselin of the Woods Hole Oceanographic Institution noted that the *Thresher* was diving in the area where the cold waters of the Nova Scotia current meet the warmer Gulf Stream flow. Under normal conditions the situation would not affect submarine operations, but abnormal conditions existed there on April 10, according to Dr. Iselin.

Heavy winds and seas in the few days before April 10 had caused different mixing conditions which produced a stronger underwater "downdraft" than usual. When the *Thresher* entered this downdraft she was physically pushed downward at a very slow speed.

Could this have been the "minor problem" the *Thresher* encountered on the morning of April 10? Dr. Iselin theorized that the effect of the downdraft could have pushed the *Thresher* down 300 feet in two minutes. But experienced submariners discount the underwater storm theory, noting submariners are used to operating in underwater currents. They also point out that, with her normal ballast-blowing and propulsion capabilities, the *Thresher* could have easily recovered from such a downdraft, if indeed she had encountered such conditions.

Enemy action may have figured in the death of the *Thresher.* Although the Navy has officially given little credence to the theory of enemy action, there are some persons who believe there may have been some enemy influence. Speculation that Soviet agents sabotaged the submarine in the shipyard or enemy frogmen attached explosive charges to the *Thresher* as she headed out to sea is generally discounted.

There is also this theory: The *Thresher* surfaced on April 10 and, because of communication trouble, was unable to contact the *Skylark*. She was then set upon by the armed crew of a Soviet trawler, captured, and taken back to the Soviet Union or scuttled. In view of the messages received by the *Skylark,* the failure to find any Soviet ships in the search area, and the later findings of the *Trieste,* this theory is considered in the category of fantasy.

But it is not impossible that the *Thresher* was being trailed on her trials by a Soviet nuclear submarine with the purpose of "spying" on the United States undersea craft. There could have been an accidental collision in which the submarines did not strike each other hard enough to recognize an underwater collision, but hard enough to cause a small hull rupture or to damage a diving plane on the *Thresher.* Such damage might have initially been evaluated as a "minor problem." Inside the *Thresher,* it might at first appear that a pipe had failed because of the sea pressure or that the diving planes had jammed. While the *Thresher* obviously broke up—as evidenced by the amount of her debris found on the ocean floor—the Soviet submarine may have also been fatally damaged and plunged straight down, penetrating the ocean floor and making the craters observed by the *Trieste* during her first series of dives. Or, the Soviet submarine might have gotten away. But no Soviet submarine was in the area—a fact confirmed by post-Cold War research—and certainly none was missing.

"A flooding casualty in the engine room is believed to be the 'most probable' cause of the sinking of the nuclear submarine USS THRESHER . . . ." Ambiguous and indefinite. Exactly what caused the worst submarine disaster in history will probably never be known with absolute certainty.

Still, a subsequent and dispassionate examination of the evidence, indicates that the initial event in the death of the *Thresher*—history's worst submarine disaster—was most probably a reactor shut-down or "scram," a term originating with the first U.S. reactor in 1942, when a "super-critical reactor ax-man" stood by to quickly cut the ropes holding the control rods in the event that the reactor went super-critical. Quickly dropping the control rods into a reactor absorbs neutrons and slows or stops the nuclear reaction.

CHAPTER 10

AFTERMATH AND AFTERTHOUGHTS

The *Thresher*'s reactor might have automatically shut down for a number of reasons, such as an electrical short circuit or even a heavy object being dropped on a nearby deck. Admiral Rickover only indirectly denied this theory. In July 1963 and again in July 1964 he testified before congressional committees about the *Thresher* loss:

> . . . statements have been made that [classified] the ship lost propulsion. Such statements cannot, in my opinion, be substantiated and may cause us to lose sight of the basic technical and management inadequacies that must be faced and solved if we are to do all we can to prevent further *Thresher* disasters.
>
> It is not the purpose of my testimony here today to prove that the nuclear power plant did not contribute to this casualty. When fact, supposition, and speculation which have been used interchangeably are properly separated, you will find that the known facts are so meager it is almost impossible to tell what was happening aboard the *Thresher* at the critical time.

Following those statements, Rickover's testimony was mainly a series of criticisms against the frequent rotation of naval officers, particularly those concerned with the *Thresher's* overhaul in the shipyard; the lack of adequate welding techniques of the critical piping that penetrated the submarine's pressure hull; the poor management and quality control in submarine construction; and the manner in which the Navy's leadership made decisions about submarine requirements.

Admiral Rickover was correct in his accusations—there were problems in all of those areas. But he carefully steered Congress and the Navy away from consideration of the nuclear plant as having any part in the submarine's loss, at least with regard to his responsibility. He carefully stated in one congressional hearing that he did not have responsibility for the *Thresher's* reactor plant "Because it was a follow-on ship. . . . The *Thresher* was essentially a *Skipjack*-type submarine except that all the equipment was mounted on resilient mounting. . . . [to reduce noise]"

Admiral Ralph K. James, Chief of the Bureau of Ships during the *Thresher's* construction, in his memoirs, wrote:

I feel from what I know of the inquiry in which I participated, what I know of the ship itself, and events that occurred up to that time that a failure of a silver soldered pipe fitting somewhere in the boat caused a discharge of a stream of water on the nuclear control board and "scrammed" the power plant.

Then, according to James,

Because of inadequate design of the nuclear controls for the plant, power on the boat was lost at a time where [*sic*] the depth of water in which the submarine was operating forced enough water into the hull that prevented her from rising again because they couldn't get power back in the boat.

Commander Axene told the author of this book that he would have reported a reactor scram as a "minor difficulty." He would not have so labeled a flooding casualty, even through a small-diameter pipe. Perhaps the flooding casualty that caused the scram was improperly reported to the control room, hence the *Thresher* reported to the *Skylark* only that there was a "minor difficulty." If there was a flooding casualty and the ship did have propulsion available, the fastest and most efficient way to surface would be to increase speed and use the diving planes to surface. That the *Thresher* could not do this was more likely the loss of propulsion through a scram than problems with her diving planes.

Loss of propulsion would have forced use of the backup surfacing system—the blowing of high-pressure air into the ballast tanks to lighten the submarine. But "attempting to blow up" undoubtedly meant that this backup surfacing system was failing. Later tests of the blow system in *Thresher*-class submarines determined that the high-pressure system was inadequate for an emergency blow from test depth. Further, in the cold depths the high-pressure air may have frozen and clogged strainers in the system.

Then, without either propulsion or an effective emergency blow system to bring the *Thresher* to the surface, the "heavy" submarine drifted downward until Lieutenant Commander Harvey announced that his ship was exceeding "test depth."

The reactor scram theory gains credence because shortly after the loss of the *Thresher* Rickover convened a group of his engineers and available submarine commanders to determine how to reduce the time needed to restart a reactor after such a shutdown. New procedures were developed to accelerate restarting the reactor in hopes of avoiding a future disaster like the loss of the *Thresher*. Admiral James and others have spoken of this effort to accelerate reactor start-ups after a scram.

Thus, there is ample—albeit not conclusive—evidence that the *Thresher* was killed by the failure of the magnificent S5W nuclear propulsion plant that had been the core of her remarkable capabilities.

The loss of the *Thresher* with 129 Navymen and civilians touched the American public deeply. Submarines and submarining, long considered a deadly business, had come to be thought of as a safe business by the early 1960s. Indeed, in the 17 years after World War II only two U.S. submarines were lost: the diesel-electric *Cochino*, sunk off Norway in the summer of 1949 after a hydrogen gas explosion, and the diesel-electric *Stickleback*, rammed and sunk by an escort ship off Hawaii in the summer of 1958. A civilian engineer aboard the *Cochino* was lost, and seven sailors from the submarine *Tusk* drowned when the latter submarine took off the *Cochino's* crew in that disaster. No men were lost when the Stickleback went down. Thus a sense of security about submarine operations grew in the American public's mind.

To be sure, there were the occasional reports of a man being swept from the bridge of a low-lying, surfaced submarine during rough weather, or of a man being killed in one of the fires that now and then flare aboard submarines. Nuclear-propelled as well as conventional diesel-electric submarines have suffered these casualties: In June 1960 the nuclear submarine *Sargo* was rocked by explosions and fire at Pearl Harbor while taking on highly unstable liquid oxygen. One of her crew died as the fire was extinguished only by flooding the aftermost compartment of the submarine. And the *Thresher's* sister submarine *Permit* was in a collision with a freighter while running submerged off the coast of California on May 9, 1962. At the time, the *Permit* was on a test run with 140 persons on board. The submarine suffered some damage, but was never in danger of sinking and no one was injured. There were other accidents and incidents.

However, incidents were still relatively infrequent, considering that by the time of the *Thresher* disaster the United States had 27 nuclear-propelled submarines and almost 100 diesel-electric submarines in service. Their dives totaled some 50,000 every year. Nuclear submarines had helped to build this image of submarine safety. Complex as they are, nuclear submarines have an additional safety factor because of their ability to run submerged and be less endangered by surface craft, and because of the extra margin of power that their nuclear power plants provide.

And, just in case a submarine did go down, in the public's mind there was that wonderful rescue chamber—commonly called the McCann chamber—that could retrieve sailors from sunken submarines. The whole nation had read about the remarkable device when it pulled 33 submarines from the clutches of death in 1939 after the *Squalus* went down.

Suddenly the world was shocked to learn that a submarine had sunk carrying 129 men to a watery death. To compound the tragedy—from a military point of view—the lost submarine was the prototype for the nation's most advanced hunter-killer craft; two identical nuclear submarines were already in service, the *Permit* and *Plunger;* more than a dozen additional ships of this class and derivatives were already under construction.

There was no question of survival for those on board the *Thresher.* The reaction of the press was universal. Reporters and columnists who normally would not consider themselves submarine-orientated, or even Navy-orientated, interrupted their normal outpouring of words on politics, labor, science, finances, sex, and the like to write about the *Thresher*. Reporters normally assigned to cover military affairs wrote column after column on the "big picture" of the nuclear-powered submarines and presented their readers with specious speculation about what had happened to the *Thresher*. "Survivors" of the *Thresher* disaster—those ashore on the day she sailed on her last voyage—were interviewed for newspapers, radio, and television.

For the families of the 129 men who were aboard the *Thresher* that day, her loss defies description here. The families of crew members, especially submarine crews, are a closely-knit group. Usually, as with most Navy families, they are far away from their real relatives. New families join the group as new men are assigned, and old families leave as their men leave the submarine for other assignments. A two- or three-year association is usual in these family groups and, especially with the men away for weeks or months at a time, there is a warm relationship. Often the families meet again after a few years when their menfolk are again assigned to duty together, and the ties between the families are drawn still tighter.

The men of this community work together at the same "office" or "factory." Their wives shop together at the same stores. All go to the same doctors. The children go to the same school and play on the same teams. This artificial family is in many ways closer than any outside the service. Everyone knows exactly what the income of everyone else is because military pay scales are in the public domain. All in the *Thresher* family faced the same problems and occasional pleasures of moving, shopping in the commissary, using Navy medical facilities, and having the same trash collector.

Without warning, more than 100 members of the *Thresher* family were killed. The impact on a small community is difficult to understand. In World War II there were a few National Guard units from small towns that were almost totally destroyed in combat; in 1963 a commercial airliner crash in France killed a host of the civic and cultural leaders of Atlanta, Georgia.

But in some ways the death of those aboard the *Thresher* was even more tragic. Husbands and sweethearts aboard her had gone out for a cruise of only a couple of days. A three-day sea trial was not a voyage. It was more akin to a three-day business meeting. Dinners were planned for the next night, tickets for shows were purchased, a broken toy was left on the table to be fixed, letters were left in the hall to be mailed the next day—the next day because going out for two nights was routine; not planned for except to put a razor, toothbrush, a tube of toothpaste, and a towel in a small bag.

How many wives in the Portsmouth area went to the door the night of April 10 wondering why her husband had knocked and not used his key and why the *Thresher* was in so early? How many wondered why the man standing there was not her husband, but another man in the same uniform her husband wore? And how many knew at once the horror of what had happened as the man who stood before her swallowed hard, and with an attempt to carefully control the inflection of his voice, said, "Now we don't know for sure. . . ." Or how many wives felt a stab of pain in their hearts as a son or daughter ran to her saying, "Mommy, mommy, the television says there's an atomic submarine sunk. . . ." These were tragic occurrences and they took place over and over again in the Portsmouth area that April night.

The men of the *Thresher* were also part of the larger family of Navy submariners who had duty together every few years. Rear Admiral Bernard A. Clarey, commander of the Pacific Fleet Submarine Force, noted: "The sudden and tragic loss of the *Thresher* with all hands has been a shocking experience. There are few submarines who did not have a friend or former shipmate on board." Most submariners now on active duty had known, served with, or gone to school with someone in the *Thresher*.

Official Navy reaction to the *Thresher's* loss was immediate and thorough. Orders went out that where possible Navymen were to visit the homes of *Thresher* crewmen to break the news of her loss and offer what assistance they could. The Navy quickly declared that the *Thresher* lost and determined "that all personnel aboard the USS *Thresher* on 10 April 1963 died on 10 April 1963." This was the equivalent of a death certificate, so necessary for the purposes of insurance and survivor benefits. The quasi-official Navy Relief Society offered immediate financial assistance to those needing it until government checks would arrive.

The *Skylark's* message sent late on the morning of April 10 set into motion a two-phase search for the *Thresher*: one to scour the seas for a surfaced submarine with a communications failure and one to attempt to find the shattered hulk of the *Thresher* on the ocean floor. As it soon became apparent that the *Thresher* had indeed been lost the latter phase became predominant. In Washington several scientists were requested to serve as the Technical Advisory Committee for the *Thresher* search. Dr. Arthur Maxwell of the Office of Naval Research was named to head the group.

The Navy also set up several special groups to address *Thresher*-related issues: The Court of Inquiry headed by Vice

Admiral Austin and a board to re-examine the design philosophy and construction characteristics of the *Thresher* class. This second group, under Retired Rear Admiral A.I. McKee, consisted of officers who were either experienced submarines or naval constructors and, in addition, were not previously associated with the design and construction of the *Thresher*. This was done to provide a relatively objective study in addition to those being made by the submarines and designers who were familiar with the *Thresher*.

After it was determined that the *Thresher* was lost, orders went out to her sister submarines *Permit* and *Plunger*, both in the Pacific Fleet, limiting the depths to which they could dive. Depth restrictions were also placed on the more advanced Polaris missile submarines, which incorporated many of the *Thresher* design features. This precautionary step was not indicative of any lack of confidence in the *Thresher* design, but rather a conservative and deliberate safety measure that would simply lower the possibility that another accident might occur during the time the Navy was trying to determine what had happened to the *Thresher*. During this period no submarine operations were halted, and construction and sea trials of new nuclear-powered submarines continued, albeit with some delays and with a greater degree of inspection.

The Navy reviewed all of its submarine operational procedures and safety precautions, developed as a result of more than 60 years of peacetime and wartime experience. Particular attention was paid to damage-control procedures. And, with submarine deep-sea trials continuing, escorting ships—normally submarine rescue ships like the *Skylark*—were ordered to tape-record all transmissions to and from submarines. Although in no way could the *Skylark* have prevented the *Thresher*'s loss or rendered any kind of assistance to her, an accurate record of the submarine's last messages might have helped to determine precisely her "minor problem."

As the design and construction of the *Thresher* were studied by the Court of Inquiry and other groups, several changes were made in submarine-building techniques. The Navy stepped up its program to improve the art of silver brazing piping. Although there was no direct evidence of a failure of a "silbraze" joint in the *Thresher*, the large number of such joints in nuclear-powered submarines made a silbraze failure a distinct possibility.

The Bureau of Ships drew up a list of alterations that were to be made on deep-diving submarines before the imposed depth limitations could be lifted. The Navy ordered careful examination of all piping and welding in submarines of this class; ballast-blowing systems, which were found incapable of bringing the submarine to the surface from deep depths, were modified; and other changes were made. These items— known collectively as the Submarine Safety or SUBSAFE package also were applied to all new construction submarines. The several unfinished *Thresher*s were delayed for SUBSAFE modifications, and three, the SSN 613–615, were lengthened 13¾ feet, in part because of SUBSAFE features, including additional buoyancy, as well as to provide larger sail structures to make space for additional masts. The SUBSAFE program would slightly increase the building time of nuclear-propelled Polaris submarines, but would not change the previously established submarine-building plans.

The Court of Inquiry heard many hours of testimony regarding quality control practices in naval shipyards. Inspection techniques and quality control measures were improved, and more improvements were made as the results of the court and various boards are studied and translated into engineering practices. Typical of these improved practices was an ultrasonic inspection technique to help assure the integrity of high-pressure piping systems in submarines.

During the search phase of the *Thresher* disaster much attention was focused on the science of oceanography. Addressing the oceanographic aspects of the *Thresher* search, Dr. Maxwell stated, . . . the work we have done on navigation [in the search area], the number of soundings that we made, this is by far the most surveyed piece of ocean bottom its size in the world, in deep water.

Now, in addition to these kind of measurements, we have a great number of measurements of currents and other oceanographic factors in the area. We are also looking into the problem of how do you find things like submarines when they are sitting on the bottom. After all, this is a Navy problem that the Navy is interested in. And here is a situation that was set up that has given us a big chance to work on the problem.

The problem of the "location, identification, rescue from and recovery of deep submerged large bodies from the ocean floor" was assigned to a study group under Rear Admiral Edward C. Stephan, the Oceanographer of the Navy and a veteran submariner. That effort would have a significant role in future naval operations (see Chapter 11).

And after every death life must go on. In the days immediately following the *Thresher*'s loss submarines around the world discussed the accident in general terms with the limited information available to them. Most submariners soon concluded that exactly what happened to the *Thresher* would probably never be known. They checked over their own operational procedures and griped a little over the depth restrictions imposed on the newer boats which deprived them of their full abilities.

Generally, there was no fear that it was dangerous to operate their submarines. No flood of resignations occurred in the submarine service. There were some, to be sure, but men are always leaving the submarine service and indeed the Navy for a variety of reasons. Perhaps the service was better off for those men who did leave.

And, the submarine service is no doubt better off for men like Lieutenant Richard H. Scales of the *Thresher's* sister submarine *Tinosa,* completed in 1964, who stayed in submarines. His wife Cynthia explained the effect of the *Thresher's* loss on her and her feelings about her husband's work in a letter to his parents:

Fear for my husband's safety in the line of duty is no greater than yours for Jack, for instance, at the wheel of his car in heavy traffic. An awareness of the risks involved is always present in both of us, but fears are kept in check by our confidence in them and in their equipment—in Dick's case, a submarine.

And, . . . the Navy of Daddy's day and the Navy of today are so dissimilar that my indoctrination into the life in general, and submarining in particular, has been as unique an experience for me as for any other civilian-born Navy wife. And I've learned to love it.

Perhaps I have little choice—Dick loves it, and I love him, and my pride in him defies expression. It's not an easy life, Heaven knows. There are days (roughly three a week since Thanksgiving) when I'd like to scuttle the whole U.S. fleet and escape to a cave on the side of an isolated mountain, just to retaste the joys of that grand old institution of togetherness known as The Family. But let a civilian aim one word of criticism at the Navy, and I fly to its defense like a lioness protecting her newborn cubs. Even now. More now, in fact, than ever before.

> To her parents-in-law she explained:
>
> There will be resignations from the submarine fleet as a direct result of the *Thresher's* tragic end. If there are men of special training and talents, such as Dick's, who can be lured back into civilian life just for the promise of personal gains in private industry, surely there are as many who'll leave in a greater hurry when they feel that their very skins are at stake. And without malice, I think that perhaps the Navy will be a stronger, stabler force for their having left it. I shouldn't have to tell you that it's not for any lack of love for Dick that I haven't even brought up the subject. For one thing, it would do absolutely no good. In truth, if I thought there were the slightest chance that a wife's selfish whining could move Dick an inch from his chosen course, I'd lose much of my respect for him. Deep inside, I think you would too.

It must also be noted that in the wake of the *Thresher* disaster no Polaris submarine patrols were curtailed; none postponed. Nuclear submarines continued to conduct deep test dives—admittedly under temporarily imposed restrictions—and additional submarines have gone to sea.

Still, more nuclear-propelled submarines have been lost, American and Soviet-Russian.

CHAPTER 11

ESCAPE AND RESCUE

Fourteen days after the *Thresher* was lost Secretary of the Navy Korth established the Deep Submergence Systems Review Group to examine all naval capabilities in the deep-ocean environment, but especially submarine escape and rescue. The term "escape" refers to the survivors of a stricken submarine reaching the surface without outside assistance; "rescue" is the use of external means to remove survivors from a stricken submarine.

Headed by Rear Admiral Edward C. Stephan, the Oceanographer of the Navy, the panel consisted of 58 experts in oceanography, under-water engineering, and submarines. Among the publicly prominent persons to serve on Admiral Stephan's panel were Retired Captain William R. Anderson, who had commanded the pioneer nuclear submarine *Nautilus*; Edwin A. Link, inventor of the famed Link aviation trainer who had turned his interests to underwater research; and Dr. Allyn Vine of the Woods Hole Oceanographic Institution. Significantly, no representative from Admiral Rickover's nuclear propulsion directorate was on the panel.

The review group completed its work in March 1964 and recommended that a major effort be made to improve the Navy's ability to recover personnel from sunken submarines, to investigate the ocean floor, to recover small objects from the ocean floor (such as weapons and satellites), to salvage sunken submarines, and to enable men to work on the ocean floor down to at least the 600-foot continental shelf, ostensibly for salvage operations. The report stressed that "Development of the capability to recover surviving personnel from disabled submarines at any depth is mandatory for humanitarian, morale, and military effectiveness reasons."

An agency to develop these capabilities was established in June 1964, named the Deep Submergence Systems Project (DSSP). It was initially within the Navy's Special Projects Office, home of the Polaris missile effort. The reason for this location this was Special Projects' expertise in managing large, complex projects, and the continued efforts by that office to assess and understand deep-ocean technologies for advanced strategic weapon systems. The man named to direct the deep-submergence effort was Dr. John P. Craven, an engineer who was chief scientist of the Polaris project. After the deep-submergence project was made an independent project office, Craven was succeeded by a naval officer as project manager, but remained as chief scientist for both Special Projects and DSSP.

The DSSP staff quickly set up five *overt* programs:

- Submarine location, escape, and rescue
- Object location and recovery
- Man-in-the-Sea (working at depths to 600 feet with the technique known as saturation diving)
- Large object salvage (i.e., submarines)
- *NR-1* nuclear-propelled research submersible

And, hidden within the organization and financial dealings of DSSP would be several covert or "black" projects, very highly classified activities that would take advantage of the technologies being developed by the open or "white" programs. For example, Operation Ivy Bells was the U.S. Navy's top-secret program to tap into Soviet seafloor communication cables in the Soviet Far East and Arctic areas. Using nuclear-propelled submarines ostensibly modified to support DSSP activities, and saturation diving techniques, Ivy Bells was a highly successful effort from 1971 until 1980, when the operation was revealed to the Soviets by American traitor Ronald Pelton, a former employee of the National Security Agency.

Submarine *location, escape,* and *rescue* were given a high— and very public—priority. The principal means of locating a sunken submarine at the time of the *Thresher* disaster was the tethered marker buoy. This was a float fitted with a light and inscribed "submarine sunk here," with a telephone inside. Submarines carried two such buoys fitted into their deck, which were be manually released from a submarine on the bottom with survivors on board. Of course, "bottom" meant above the collapse depth of the submarine, while the cable anchoring the buoy to the submarine was only a few hundred feet long. Below that depth, if the submarine was intact and there were survivors, possibly the UQC acoustic could be used if electric power was available, or the crew could tap on the hull with wrenches or hammers. Neither sound would transmit very far, and certainly not to a searching aircraft.

DSSP immediately began the development of various electronic beacons and markers that would help to locate a disabled submarine at virtually any depth regardless of whether there or not were survivors. These battery operated devices would be ejected from the submarine, float to the surface, and send out a pre-recorded radio call for help; and, there would be improved signaling devices on the submarine. The small antenna would limit their range. Further, their use was questionable because of the fear that in a combat situation a near miss by an enemy weapon or actual damage to the submarine could cause these emergency devices to reveal its exact location to an enemy.

More realistic to the needs of survivors were the "escape" efforts developed by DSSP to enable survivors to escape from a partially flooded submarine. Submarine escape dates to at least 1851. Wilhelm Bauer, a corporal of Bavarian artillery, constructed a submarine of iron plates that was propelled by a hand-operated propeller. It dived by taking water into tanks and a moveable weight slid forward to give the craft a diving angle.

Bauer's submarine, named *Der Brandtaucher,* came to an untimely end when the weight slid too far forward during trials off Kiel on February 1, 1851. The craft plunged out of control to the bottom, some 60 feet down. The clear-thinking Bauer sought to flood the disabled craft so that he could open the hatch against the outside water pressure and swim to the surface. It took Bauer almost five hours to convince his two crewmen to allow flooding of the craft. Finally convincing them, all three men safely reached the surface. It was history's first submarine escape.

(Bauer subsequently interested the Russian government in his ideas and built a highly successful submarine, *La Diable Marin,* at St. Petersburg in 1955. He made 134 dives in the craft before it was lost.)

Early in the twentieth century several navies developed emergency breathing devices to help survivors escape from stricken submarines. The U.S. Navy in 1929 adopted the Momsen lung, developed by then-Lieutenant Charles (Swede)

Momsen. In his book *Hell at 50 Fathoms,* Vice Admiral Charles Lockwood wrote, "My frequent complaint was that Momsen was just as full of ideas as a dog is of fleas—and that he continually brought them over and turned them loose on my desk. But they were smart, constructive ideas. . . ."

The Momsen lung consisted of a mouthpiece, two tubes, a clip, and a breathing bag, the last being strapped to the man's chest. The wearer held the mouthpiece in his teeth and put the clip on his nose. He then inhaled oxygen-enriched air from the lung through one tube and exhaled through the other tube. The lung was charged with oxygen from the submarine's high-pressure oxygen system just before the man exited the submarine. Once on the surface the lung could provide limited floatation.

Although the U.S. Navy trained submariners extensively in using the Momsen lung, its use was fraught with danger. Too rapid ascent would induce air embolisms or "bends," which were painful and possibly fatal; there was no protection from water temperature; and there was no means of flotation when on the surface.

The Momsen lung was used only once in an actual submarine escape. On her fifth patrol during World War II the submarine *Tang* was operating in the Formosa Strait during October 1944. She had sunk seven Japanese cargo ships on the patrol. On the night of the October 24–25 her initial attack damaged a Japanese destroyer and transport. Running on the surface, the *Tang*'s skipper, Commander Richard H. O'Kane, re-attacked the transport with two torpedoes. The first ran straight to its mark; the second torpedo made a sudden turn and headed back toward the *Tang*. O'Kane attempted to avoid the torpedo, but it struck the submarine's stern.

O'Kane and eight other men on the conning tower were thrown into the water. Four managed to stay afloat until morning when they were taken aboard a Japanese ship. The *Tang* plunged to the ocean floor, a depth of 180 feet. Inside the submarine the survivors burned code books and other classified publications. Continued Japanese depth-charging exacerbated the desperate condition of the survivors, with fires eating up oxygen within the submarine.

Thirteen men donned Momsen lungs and attempted to escape through the *Tang's* forward escape hatch. Eight reached the surface, the others becoming trapped in the escape chamber. Five of those who made the ascent were able to stay afloat until morning. In all, nine men, including O'Kane, were taken aboard Japanese ships, where they were beaten savagely.

After the war O'Kane was presented the Medal of Honor by President Truman while the *Tang* became one of only three U.S. warships to receive two Presidential unit Citations during the war. (During the *Tang's* five war patrols she was the second highest-scoring U.S. submarine in terms of number and tonnage of Japanese ships sunk.)

After the war the Momsen lung continued in U.S. Navy service. Clearly an improved method of submarine escape was needed. The Navy began experimenting with the so-called buoyant ascent technique, wherein the man exited the submarine without a breathing device and simply purged air from their lungs or "blew" out air all the way to the surface. This technique was adopted in 1956 and specially qualified U.S. Navy personnel made an open-sea ascent from 320 feet and British submariners successfully ascended 475 feet. Captain George Bond, a Navy medical officer, who led the U.S. Navy's efforts in these buoyant ascents, described coming up from 320 feet as "wonderful." He reported that it took approximately 25 seconds to pressurize the submarine escape chamber so that he could open the escape hatch, about 12 more seconds for Bond and his companion to check their inflatable life vests, and 57 seconds to reach the surface.

Bond believed that such escapes—for specially trained personnel—would be feasible from depths of 600 feet. Meanwhile, for use throughout the submarine force, a hooded life jacket, called the Steinke hood for Lieutenant Harris Steinke, was adopted to help provide buoyancy and help self-discipline during the ascent. This procedure was simulation tested to depths of 450 feet.

However, after examining the device in the wake of the *Thresher* loss the Stephen review group declared:

> Survival after escape depends upon favorable surface conditions and timely pickup by surface ships or aircraft. Escape from deep water requires a high degree of competence and confidence which can only be achieved by extensive training. The risks and time required have limited escape training to date *so that escape from below 50 feet is only speculative.* [Emphasis added]

The DSSP organization sought to adopt British escape "suits" that provided for both buoyant ascent, thermal protection in the water, and survival on the surface for use aboard U.S. submarines. These suits would enable survivors to escape if a submarine was sunk at depths to some 600 feet. But the collapse depths of American submarines built after World War II—even the diesel-electric submarines—were much greater. Thus, an advanced rescue system was needed.

The McCann submarine rescue chamber had a greater operating depth—in theory. Developed primarily by "Swede" Momsen and Lieutenant Commander Allen McCann, this was a diving bell or chamber lowered from a surface ship to the submarine's escape hatch. A hatch in the bottom of the McCann chamber could "mate" with the submarine hatch and both then opened to permit passage between the two.

Significantly, the McCann chamber was lowered from a surface ship. This meant that after the disabled submarine was located the ship had to be within range of the stricken submarine before the survivors' air was exhausted, or they died of carbon dioxide poisoning, or hyperthermia, or other causes. Heavy weather could prevent the rescue ship from mooring over the stricken submarine or sending down divers, who are required to attach the chamber's hauldown cable to the submarine escape hatch. And, the submarine could be lying at too great an angle and thus prevent the chamber from successfully mating with the hatch. Of course, there was no under-ice capability.

The nine-ton chamber itself was designed to carry eight submarine survivors in addition to two operators. It's operating depth was 850 feet although its predicted collapse depth of 1,200 feet meant that in an emergency it could be sent to that depth.

McCann chambers began entering U.S. Navy service in 1930. Several exercises were carried out with the chamber, but its first—and only—operational use came in May 1939 when the newly built submarine *Squalus* departed the Portsmouth Navy Yard for sea trails. On board was a crew of 56 under Lieutenant Oliver Naquin and three civilians.

A mechanical failure led to the engine room flooding and sending the submarine plunging to the ocean floor. Coming to rest at a depth of 240 feet, Naquin quickly determined that the after section of the submarine was flooded with the 26 men in those compartments undoubtedly dead. Thirty-three men were still alive. Subsequently, distress flares fired from the

Squalus caught the attention of her sister submarine *Sculpin*, on the surface searching for her sister ship. The *Sculpin* located the rescue buoy and there was a brief telephone conversation with sunken submarine before the cable broke.

A flotilla of ships was sent to assist the stricken *Squalus*, including the rescue ship *Falcon*, which was carrying a rescue chamber. With great difficulty the *Squalus* was located, divers sent down to attach the down-haul cable, and the McCann chamber descended into the depths.

In three successful trips down to the *Squalus* the McCann chamber brought up 25 survivors. Lieutenant Naquin and seven others remained as the chamber descended on its fourth dive. It was dark on the surface as well as in the depths. At 8:24 p.m. on May 24 the last survivors had entered the chamber and the ascent began. But 160 feet from the surface the chamber came to a halt as the cable jammed. The chamber was slowly lowered to the ocean floor and divers were dispatched to try to free the cable, but without success.

Cold or oxygen starvation would soon kill the ten men trapped in the chamber. Finally, aboard the *Falcon*, Momsen and McCann decided that they might be able to haul in the chamber by hand—very slowly and very carefully. It took only 20 minutes to haul in the cable and, at 12:23 a.m. the chamber broke the surface. Naquin and the other seven survivors had spent 36 hours entombed in the submarine and just over four hours entrapped in the McCann chamber.

As Rear Admiral Stephan's review group examined the *Squalus* experience and the McCann chamber's capabilities and limitations, it was obvious that a new rescue system was needed, one that could provide more rapid response over great distances, operate regardless of surface weather conditions or ice, and save crewmen from much greater depths.

The review group recommended the development of small, manned submersibles that could be transported long distances by aircraft, and carried to the disaster scene by specially designed surface ships or nuclear-propelled submarines. If carried by a submarine, the Deep Submergence Rescue Vehicle (DSRV) could "take off" from a submerged submarine and travel down to the disable craft, mate with escape hatches to take aboard survivors, and return to the "mother submarine."

Each DSRV would carry 12 survivors in addition to two operators. The review group proposed six DSRV rescue units to be based at various locations, each with two vehicles. The DSRV would have an operating depth of 3,500 feet—much greater than the collapse depth of the *Thresher*, the Navy's newest submarine design.

Two factors soon contributed to a major change in the DSRV program. First, DSSP determined that a larger, more-capable rescue vehicle could be built that would carry 24 survivors plus three crewmen. This led to the decision to procure only six vehicles, to be based at three locations, probably bases on the U.S. East Coast and West Coast, and at Pearl Harbor. (This three-base arrangement, it was estimated by the Navy, would enable a DSRV to reach almost 50 percent of the "probable" submarine disasters in which rescue was feasible within 24 hours; almost all of the other locations could be reached within 50 hours.)

Second, DSSP was initiating the various deep submergence programs as the United States was engaged in a large-scale and expensive war in Vietnam. Planned funding for the project was cut and cut again until, in the event, only two DSRVs were procured—the DSRV-1, later named *Mystic*, completed in 1971 and the DSRV-2, named *Avalon*, completed in 1972.

The DSRV consists of three interconnected personnel spheres, each 7½ feet in diameter, constructed of HY-140 steel, encased in a fiberglass-reinforced plastic shell. The forward sphere contains the vehicle's controls and is manned by a pilot and co-pilot; the center and after spheres can accommodate 24 survivors and a third crewman. The survivors could be transferred directly from the stricken submarine to the DSRV and then to a mother submarine or to the surface rescue ship without exposure to the open sea. The *Mystic* originally was certified only to operate down to 3,500 feet for technical reasons; subsequently both she and the *Avalon* were rated at 5,000 feet.

The two DSRVs were based at the North Island Naval Air Station in San Diego, California, where they could be quickly loaded into C-5 transport aircraft and flown to forward bases, or loaded aboard San Diego-based nuclear submarines. Two large, specially configured submarine rescue ships also were built to carry the DSRV. Periodically the DSRVs were flown to other bases in the United States and overseas to participate in rescue exercises. Several British and French as well as U.S. submarines were modified to carry and support a DSRV.

When one DSRV was "standing alert" at North Island the other would be employed in exercises, undergo overhaul, or possibly be engaged in clandestine search, recovery, and related operations. The use of a mother submarine to transport the DSRV would facilitate such activities.

However, the development of advanced submarine location, escape, and rescue systems—even had they been available—would not have helped those aboard the *Thresher.* Nor could they help the 99 officers and enlisted men in the second U.S. submarine to be lost, the *Scorpion.*

CHAPTER 12

ANOTHER SUBMARINE IS MISSING

One year after the *Thresher* was lost, writing in the U.S. Navy's professional magazine, the Naval Institute *Proceedings*, Vice Admiral E.W. Grenfell wrote:

Mr. Polmar predicts that we will again suffer submarine losses similar to *Thresher*. I believe what he means to point out is that, in the statistical abstract context, if we operate "X" number of submarines, we are bound to suffer "Y" number of casualties. I find that I cannot accept this premise, other than in the purely abstract sense.

Grenfell, as commander of the Atlantic Fleet Submarine Force, helped to develop and enforce policies and procedures to the insure that the "abstract premise" that the United States would again lose a nuclear submarine would not occur. There were problems in the submarine force, accidents and "incidents," a term applied to problems related to nuclear propulsion plants. The nuclear submarines *Sargo* and *Shark* had both suffered major fires; these were sister ships to a submarine named *Scorpion*.

A little more than five years after the *Thresher* disaster the Submarine Force headquarters in Norfolk sent out the message "SUBMISS"—Submarine Missing. The nuclear-propelled submarine *Scorpion* had failed to report her pending arrival at Norfolk. This time families already were on the pier, waiting for "daddy's boat" to steam into view.

The *Scorpion* was one of six *Skipjack*-class attack submarines completed from 1959 to 1961, the immediate predecessors to the *Thresher* design. The *Skipjacks* introduced the definitive S5W reactor plant to submarines and were the first nuclear submarines to have the *Albacore* hull, resulting in a 33-knot submarine, America's fastest until the mid-1970s. The *Scorpion*, built by Electric Boat at Groton, Connecticut, joined the fleet in 1960. The 252-foot submarine displaced 3,500 tons submerged, thus she was smaller than the *Thresher*. The added size of the newer design provided a greater operating depth, more quieting, and more sonar capability than in the *Skipjacks*.

Unlike the new *Thresher*, the *Scorpion* was tried and tested. She had made her first overseas deployment, to the Mediterranean, in August 1960. She subsequently made additional overseas deployments plus local training operations, being based at Norfolk. Although she was in the yard several times after the SUBSAFE package was developed in 1963–1964, the *Scorpion* had not been given the full safety update. (The emergency radio transmitter buoys proposed by Admiral Stephen's review group in the wake of the *Thresher* loss had not been produced.)

On February 14, 1968 the *Scorpion* again departed Norfolk for a deployment to the Mediterranean. Under Commander Francis A. Slattery, the *Scorpion* carried 101 officers, enlisted men, and intelligence specialists. On board were 23 torpedoes; in addition to a load of 14 Mk 37 and seven older Mk 14 conventional torpedoes, there were two Mk 45 ASTOR torpedoes with nuclear warheads.

The *Scorpion* carried out regular operations with the Sixth Fleet in the Mediterranean, including operating against Soviet warships during the continuing confrontation between the two Cold War enemies. On April 28 the *Scorpion* departed the port of Naples, assigned to carry out surveillance against Soviet ships near the Canary Islands, which lie about 300 miles off northwest Africa, and then return home. En route she stopped off the U.S. naval base at Rota, near Cadiz, Spain, to transfer a crewman and an intelligence specialist ashore.

She then turned toward the Canary Islands. The Soviet ships—two hydrographic survey ships, a submarine rescue ship, and an Echo II (Project 675) nuclear submarine—were carrying out operations that interested the U.S. intelligence community. U.S. aircraft periodically flew over the ships, but perhaps the *Scorpion* would be more successful in ascertaining the nature of their activities.

On the evening of May 21 the *Scorpion* ran near the surface to radio her observations. At the time she was about 50 nautical miles south of the Azores. She then dived to a transit depth—perhaps 200 feet-and turned westward, expected to transit at a speed of 18 to 20 knots and to arrive at Norfolk at 1 p.m. local time on May 27.

At that time transiting submarines normally slowed and came near the surface once or twice a day to receive messages, it being necessary to raise an antenna above the water. And, submarines arriving in the United States from an overseas deployment generally communicated a day or so before their planned arrival to confirm their position and to receive pier assignments or changes. Radio messages were sent to the

Scorpion on May 23. They were repeated over the next two days. There was no acknowledgement.

Perhaps the submarine had suffered a radio failure, although there were backup radios. Certainly the *Scorpion* had suffered her share of breakdowns during her Mediterranean deployment. David B. Stone, a machinist's mate second class, had written home on April 12 that "we have repaired, replaced, or jury-rigged every piece of equipment" in the submarine. Hydraulic oil leaks in the sail-mounted diving planes and periscope systems plagued the submarine during her deployment. While en route to the Mediterranean she had suffered a rudder failure. Also, just before the *Scorpion* departed Norfolk she was found to have a "minor hull crack," which was not considered a safety concern.

At Norfolk, Vice Admiral Arnold F. Schade, commander of Atlantic Fleet submarines, asked that Navy ships and planes crossing the predicted track of the *Scorpion* keep a lookout for the errant submarine. Shortly after 12 noon on May 27, with the *Scorpion* expected to be on the surface approaching the entrance to Chesapeake Bay, the submarine force headquarters began broadcasting the *Scorpion*'s call name . . . "Brandywine." Again and again it was repeated. There was no response.

Most of the *Scorpion* families were at the Norfolk submarine piers by 1 p.m. Carefully, with concern, at first naval officers told the families that the *Scorpion* was running late and that they should go home. Soon, however, the families were told that the *Scorpion* was "overdue." On June 5 the term "and presumed lost" was officially added, the terminology of a submarine sunk.

Extensive air, surface, and submarine searches were undertaken along the *Scorpion*'s expected track home. Unlike the *Thresher*, she had been sailing alone. The recordings of the

Navy's seafloor Sound Surveillance System (SOSUS) system were carefully examined to ascertain if any noises related to a possible submarine sinking could be detected. Also checked were records of an Air Force hydrophone array in the Atlantic.

On May 31 sounds were identified on the acoustic printouts that indicated a possible explosion had occurred in the depths along the *Scorpion's* predicted track on May 22, 18 hours after the *Scorpion's* last radio transmission and some 400 nautical miles westward of that position. Further, the data indicated that the explosion was followed 26 seconds later by the apparent sounds of submarine bulkheads collapsing. The depth of water was some 11,100 feet. The *Scorpion* had a test depth of 700 feet and a theoretical collapse depth of 1,050 feet.

The naval research ship *Mizar* was quickly dispatched to the scene, arriving in mid-June. Trailing a camera into the depths, she began taking thousands of photos of the ocean floor in the area. The remains of the *Scorpion* were located; the hull was far more intact than the shattered remains of the *Thresher*. Subsequently, the deep-diving bathyscaph *Trieste*, greatly updated from the configuration used in the original *Thresher* search, was employed to closely observe the submarine's remains. There was some visible damage, most prominently the stern section had been forced into the amidships hull by the massive water pressure.

This time there were no UQC messages—even garbled—to help the Navy's Court of Inquiry, which was again chaired by Vice Admiral Bernard L. Austin, now retired. After six months of hearings, the court reported that the cause of the death of the *Scorpion* with all 99 men on board could not be "ascertained from any evidence now available" and that "no inconvertible proof of the exact cause" could be found.

However, in listing possible causes, the classified report of the court—released in 1993—listed torpedo accidents as the first three "probable" causes of her loss. The first, explosive sound from the *Scorpion* was calculated to have occurred west of the subsequent events. This meant that the *Scorpion* was traveling in an *easterly* direction at the time of her loss. Many submarine officers interpreted this to be a problem with one of the Mk 37 torpedoes. It may have started running while in the torpedo room or in a torpedo tube; the crew may have tried to launch it or shut it down while in the room or tube. After a certain number of propeller revolutions the torpedo would arm itself. Then a blow on the warhead or possibly other "influences" could detonate the weapon.

After the loss of the submarine *Tang* in World War II and other torpedo incidents, the Navy had designed torpedoes to automatically shut down if they made a 170-degree turn, so that they would not double back and strike the launching submarine. If the *Scorpion* had a "hot running" torpedo within the submarine or stuck in a tube, Commander Slattery would undoubtedly have turned the submarine to make the torpedo's guidance system believe that it had made a U-turn. The Mk 37 torpedo had suffered several problems in service. Indeed, on December 5, 1967, during a lengthy series of torpedo firings, the *Scorpion* had suffered a Mk 37–1 exercise torpedo malfunction with the weapon inadvertently starting up in a tube. Then, due to personnel error, it was improperly launched. (During the same firing series an unarmed Mk 45–1 ASTOR torpedo also was improperly launched; however, 27 of the *Scorpion* torpedo launches functioned properly during the period from October to December 1967.)

On the return voyage to Norfolk the submarine's crew would have been disarming all torpedoes in preparation for them being offloaded prior to entering the shipyard. Could a Mk 37 torpedo have malfunctioned and its warhead detonated before the turn was fully achieved, or had the cutoff mechanism failed? The Court of Inquiry noted that "There are ways in which one or more warheads could have been detonated including an uncontrollable fire in the Torpedo Room." The Court's report "suggested" the most probably cause of a torpedo failure:

1. A Mark 37 torpedo in a tube in fully ready condition, without propeller guard starts a "hot run" due to inadvertent activation of the battery.
2. The ship begins a turn to attempt shutdown of the propulsion motor by means of the anti-circular run device.
3. Acting on impulse, and perhaps influenced by successful ejection of a Mark 37 exercise shot which was running hot in the tube December 1967, the torpedo was released from the tube, became fully armed, and sought its nearest target, SCORPION.

As proper, the Court looked into other possible causes of the *Scorpion* loss—fire, weapons handling accident, collision, sabotage, irrational act by a crewman, flooding due to structural or personnel failure, and loss of ship control. But the Court concluded, that the most probable explanation was a torpedo detonation within or outside of the submarine.

Almost hidden in the Court of Inquiry report—under structural failure—was mention of a propeller shaft failure. But this group of causes was dismissed with the statement "None of these are considered likely as causes of serious flooding." But several submarine officers, upon reviewing all available data, have come to believe that a propeller shaft failure was the casualty that caused the death of the *Scorpion*.

Her sister ship *Scamp* had suffered a propeller shaft failure in December 1961. The following January the *Scorpion*'s shaft was replaced as a precaution. Six years later, shortly before leaving for the Mediterranean on her final deployment, a propeller shaft leak was detected and fully repaired by the submarine tender *Orion* at Norfolk.

But, according to proponents of this theory, all of the known facts "fit." And, it explains a periscope being raised, the after engine room hatch being open, the remains of a sailor in a lifejacket who may have been attached to the submarine by safety line when she briefly reached the surface, and a mooring line streamed out of the deck locker. This theory had the propeller shaft beginning to work loose, causing massive flooding; the submarine rapidly surfaces and sailors go on deck in an effort to bend a line around the shaft to stop it from pulling out completely.

As the steel shaft, 16 inches in diameter, began to work loose, it would have admitted a tremendous amount of water, even with the submarine near the surface. The *Scorpion*'s engine room would have been the worst location for flooding from considerations of stability.

Over the years other submarines have suffered shaft failures. (The nuclear-propelled *Tullibee* lost her propeller shaft while steaming submerged at a shallow depth in the Mediterranean in 1978.)

Again, the precise cause of the *Scorpion*'s loss will never be known. The first event recorded by the acoustic sensors may have been an explosion. This initiated uncontrollable flooding, according to the report of the Court of Inquiry. Twenty-six seconds later one or both reactor compartment bulkheads collapsed. The submarine plunged deeper. Sixty-five seconds later more bulkheads were heard collapsing and the *Scorpion* was believed to have fully flooded before reach the predicted hull collapse depth of 1,050 feet. Enclosed spaces outside of the pressure hull-hard ballast tanks, escape trunks, torpedo tubes-imploded. The last sounds recorded from the *Scorpion* came three minutes, ten seconds after the initial sound.

A second nuclear-propelled submarine had been lost. Still more nuclear undersea craft would go down, but they would not be American.

During the Cold War the Soviet Union lost four nuclear-propelled submarines. A fifth Soviet-built nuclear undersea craft went down after the Cold War ended and that one—the *Kursk*—had an unprecedented blaze of publicity. In addition, the Soviet Union lost several submarines with diesel-electric and closed-cycle propulsion. (The United States had lost two diesel-electric submarines during the Cold War, the *Cochino* and *Stickleback*). One of the Soviet diesel-electric submarine losses is particularly noteworthy, the *K-129*.

The Soviet Union developed and deployed ballistic missile-carrying submarines before the U.S. *Polaris* went to sea. The Soviets sent to sea both nuclear and diesel-electric submarines with ballistic missiles. These included 22 submarines of the Project 629 design, given the NATO codename Golf, completed from 1959 to 1962. The Golf-class submarines were diesel-electric propelled. Each carried three short-range, 350-nautical mile ballistic missiles, later updated to 755-nautical mile, underwater-launch weapons. All of the ballistic missiles carried nuclear warheads.

The *K-129*, a rearmed Golf II submarine, departed Kamchatka Bay (Petropavlovsk) on the Soviet Union's Pacific coast on February 25, 1968 for a missile patrol in the North Pacific. In addition to her three nuclear missiles, the submarine was armed with torpedoes, two of which had nuclear warheads. The *K-129* was manned by a crew of 97.

En route to patrol in the area of latitude 48° North and longitude 180°, on 8 March 1968 the *K-129* suffered an internal explosion and plunged to the ocean floor, a depth of three miles. The U.S. Navy's SOSUS detected the explosion, providing a specific search area of several hundred square miles and the special-purpose submarine *Halibut* was sent out to clandestinely seek the remains of the *K-129* with a deep-towed camera. Once the precise location of the *K-129* was determined, the U.S. Central Intelligence Agency in 1974 used the specially built salvage ship *Glomar Explorer* to lift the stricken submarine, which was relatively intact. The *Glomar Explorer's* purpose and special features were highly secret; she was constructed using the cover story of a seafloor mining operation under the aegis of eccentric millionaire Howard Hughes.

The clandestine *K-129* salvage effort—codename Jennifer—succeeded in raising the submarine, but was unable to bring it all up to the surface as during the lift operation the hull split with most of the craft falling back to the ocean floor. The bow section (compartments 1 and 2)—containing two nuclear as well as conventional torpedoes and the remains of six sailors—was brought aboard the *Glomar Explorer*, minutely examined, dissected, and then disposed of. The sailors' remains were recommitted to the sea in a steel chamber on September 4, 1974, with appropriate ceremony. Project Jennifer was the deepest salvage operation ever attempted.

Most Western intelligence analysts believe that personnel failure probably was the cause of the loss of the *K-129*; of her crew of 97 almost 40 were new to the submarine. Some Soviet officials contend that the *K-129* was sunk in a collision with the trailing U.S. nuclear submarine *Swordfish*, but available evidence does not support that theory.

The first Soviet nuclear submarine loss had occurred earlier, in 1970. Project 627 was the Soviet designation for the nation's first nuclear submarine class, given the NATO codename November. These were high-speed, deep-diving, heavily armed torpedo-attack submarines. Thirteen were delivered from 1958 through 1964.

On April 9, 1970, as Soviet naval forces were conducting a multi-ocean exercise known as *Okean* (Ocean), the November-class submarine *K-8* suffered an engineering casualty as a spark ignited a fire in the air regeneration system while she was operating submerged in the Atlantic, off Cape Finisterre, Spain. The submarine was able to reach the surface, but smoke and carbon dioxide forced most of the crew onto deck. Soon the ship was drifting without power.

After three days on the surface with the crew attempting to save the *K-8* in the face of strong gales, the submarine plunged into the depths on April 12. Other Soviet ships saved half of her crew of 104; 52 men were lost, including her commanding officer. Thirty men were lost with the submarine and 22 died in the water of exposure. Of those lost in the submarine, 12 were trapped in the after portion of the hull (aft of the burning No. 7 compartment); the aftermost bulkhead was penetrated by poisonous gases and the aftermost escape hatch could not be opened. This first Soviet nuclear submarine loss occurred seven years after the USS *Thresher* was lost. Although several Soviet nuclear submarines had suffered major casualties, none had sunk until the *K-8*.

The next Soviet nuclear submarine loss was unique in that the submarine *sank twice!* Project 670 (NATO Charlie) submarines were armed with cruise missiles as well as torpedoes, the missiles primarily for attacking U.S. aircraft carriers. Seventeen of these submarines were built.

The *K-429* sank in shallow water east of Petropavlovsk in the Far East on June 24, 1983 with the loss of 16 crewmen. She was salvaged and rehabilitated, but as a dockside training ship the *K-429* sank again on September 13, 1985—and was again salvaged. She was discarded in 1986.

Like the U.S. Navy's Polaris, the Soviets also constructed large, ballistic missile submarines. The first, Project 667A (NATO Yankee), went to sea in 1967, almost eight years after the first Polaris submarine, the *George Washington*, was completed. Series production of Project 667A submarines followed and, like their U.S. counterparts, they soon deployed on a continuous basis to provide a highly survivable strategic striking force. Most Soviet ballistic missiles had liquid-propellants. These were far more volatile than the solid-propellant Polaris and later U.S. missiles and several Soviet submarines suffered missile accidents. One was the *K-219*, which in 1979 suffered a missile fuel leak, a fire, and an explosion while at sea. The ship survived and a well-trained crew brought her back to port. She was repaired, although the damaged missile tube—one of 16—was not rehabilitated.

The *K-219* suffered another missile fuel accident while submerged, on patrol some 600 nautical miles off Bermuda on October 3, 1986. The ship came to the surface "but the crew could not handle the fire. Moreover, unskilled actions led to the sinking of the ship and the death of [four] men," according to an account by Soviet naval officers. A Soviet merchant ship tried, unsuccessfully, to tow the submarine and then took aboard the survivors when she went down on October 6. Four crewmen went down with the *K-219*.

Less than three years later still another Soviet nuclear submarine plunged into the ocean depths. This was the *Komsomolets* (Project 685/NATO Mike), in many respects the world's most advanced submarine at the time. The *Komsomolets* was built to evaluate several advanced technologies while being given a full combat capability. She had a titanium hull that enabled her to reach a test depth of 3,345 feet—a greater depth than any other combat submarine in the world. (The deepest diving U.S. submarine is the small, unarmed diesel-electric research craft *Dolphin*; she is rated at 3,000 feet.)

The *Komsomolets* was completed in 1984 and carried out extensive research cruises. On February 28, 1989 a second crew trained to operate the *Komsomolets* took her to sea on a combat patrol into the North Atlantic. This crew was poorly organized; for example, "the crew lacked a damage control division as a full-fledged combat unit," according to the deputy chief designer of the submarine. The crew lacked the experience of having been aboard the *Komsomolets* for four years as had the first crew.

The *Komsomolets* was at sea for 39 days. In her forward torpedo room were conventional weapons and two nuclear torpedoes. On the morning of April 7, 1989, while in the Norwegian Sea returning to her base on the Kola Peninsula, fire erupted in the seventh compartment. The flames burned out the valve of the high-pressure air supply in the compartment and the additional air—under pressure—fed the conflagration. Attempts to flood the compartment with chemicals to extinguish the fire failed and temperatures soon reached about 2,000°F.

The alarm was spread and the submarine, cruising at about 500 feet, was brought to the surface. Seals, cableways, and aluminum were destroyed in the seventh compartment and the fire spread. One seaman died in the fire. The crew fought to save the ship for six hours with the submarine beginning to flood aft. Captain 1st Rank Ye.A. Vanin, the commanding officer, ordered most crewmen onto the sea-swept deck casing and sail. The men on deck watched sections of the submarine's rubber-like coatings slide off of the hull as they melted from the intense heat within the after portion of the submarine.

Vanin was forced to order the submarine abandoned. Two rafts, housed in the casing, were launched into the frigid sea, the water temperature being near freezing. After ordering his crew off, Vanin went back into the sinking *Komsomolets*. Apparently some men had not heard the order and still were below. With four other officers and warrant officers, Vanin entered the escape chamber in the sail of the submarine as the *Komsomolets* slipped beneath the waves, stern first at an angle of some 80 degrees. Beginning in the 1960s most Soviet nuclear submarines were fitted with escape chambers that, should a submarine begin to sink or come to rest above its collapse depth, the entire crew could enter the compartment that would float up to the surface.

Water entered the escape chamber and the men had difficulty securing the lower hatch and preparing it for release. Toxic gases also entered the chamber (probably carbon monoxide). Their efforts were made to release the chamber, but failed. Then, as the craft plunged toward the ocean floor 5,250 feet below, the chamber broke free and shot to the surface. There the internal pressure blew the catches on the upper hatch. The gases had caused four men, including Vanin, to lose consciousness. One officer escaped as the rough seas washed over the chamber, flooding it and sending it plunging into the depths carrying the unconscious Vanin and three others.

The ordeal for the survivors of the *Komsomolets* was not over. Aircraft overflew the sinking submarine and dropped a life raft, and ships were en route to the scene, some 100 nautical miles south of Bear Island. An hour after the *Komsomolets* disappeared a fishing craft pulled 30 men from the sea. Of 69 men aboard the submarine that morning, 39 already were lost. The effects of freezing water and smoke eventually would take the lives of three more to bring the death toll to 42.

Less than two years after the loss of the *Komsomolets* the Soviet Union imploded. The armed forces were in large part dismantled, with major cutbacks in naval ships, aircraft, personnel, and funding. Whereas during the latter stages of the Cold War the Soviet Navy maintained air, surface, and submarine forces in many ocean areas, especially the Mediterranean, by the late 1990s forward deployments were undertaken but rarely. On August 12, 2000, Soviet naval forces were holding exercises in the Barents Sea in preparation for a deployment to the Mediterranean, among them the submarine *Kursk*.

The *Kursk* was a Project 949 (NATO Oscar) submarine, the ultimate cruise missile submarine and—after Project 941/Typhoon—the world's largest undersea craft. The *Kursk* was just over 508 feet long and displaced some 24,500 tons submerged, seven times the displacement of the *Thresher*. In addition to a massive torpedo armament, she carried 24 large, long-range, anti-ship cruise missiles. The normal crew of the Soviet submarine was 107 officers and enlisted men.

When the *Kursk* went to sea in August 2000 she also had on board 11 staff officers and two torpedo specialists for a total of 118 men (with some crewmen having been left ashore). The fleet exercises began, with two U.S. nuclear-propelled submarines and a surface sonar surveillance ship some distance from the Soviet ships, attempting to monitor their workup for the Mediterranean deployment.

Suddenly and without warning, two explosions ripped open the bow of the *Kursk*, sending her plunging to the ocean floor, a depth of 355 feet. The apparent cause of the disaster was a low-order torpedo fuel explosion within the forward torpedo room, followed two minutes, 15 seconds later by the massive detonation of one or more torpedo warheads.

All 118 men on board died, with 23 of them in after compartments surviving for some hours and perhaps days before they ultimately succumbed to cold, pressure, or toxic gases. Crude rescue efforts failed to save any of those trapped, and two men who attempted to individual escapes were found drowned in the escape trunk. (The *Kursk*'s rescue chamber and the sail structure was wrecked by the second explosion in the forward section of the submarine.) Notes found on some of 12 bodies that were later removed from the hulk told of their desperate hours awaiting their fate in the dark, cold after section of the giant submarine.

The *Kursk*, ripped apart by the two explosions, sank quickly. All four previous Soviet nuclear-propelled submarines that had sunk at sea had suffered casualties while submerged, but were able to reach the surface, where many of their crews had been able to survive. That effort was due in part to their high reserve buoyancy; obviously, the damage to the *Kursk* by the two explosions was too sudden and too catastrophic to enable the giant craft to survive even briefly.

The major question was what had caused the initial explosion. Soviet officials immediately claimed that one of the U.S. submarines "shadowing" the exercise had collided with the *Kursk*. Considering the relative sizes of the two submarines, it would be unlikely that a U.S. undersea craft could inflict major damage without herself being heavy damaged. No such damaged has been observed on the U.S. submarines. Another theory was that the *Kursk* had detonated a World War II-era mine, a type that are still found in Russian coastal waters. (Such a mine probably sank the Soviet battleship *Novorossiisk* in 1955.)

Most foreign analysts as well as many Russian experts believe that the fuel in one of the torpedoes aboard the *Kursk* exploded. That initiated a fire that detonated more nuclear warheads. The ensuing blast, possible flash of fire, and wall of water smashed through the forward portion of the submarine, killing all in their path. Probably the shielding and bulk of the *Kursk*'s two reactors prevented devastation of the after section of the submarine.

There, 23 men survived briefly, but the hull was distorted, admitting water, building up pressure, and without heat or oxygen, their lives were measured in hours. Thus perished another nuclear submarine-the seventh to be lost in the 46 years since the USS *Nautilus* first got underway on nuclear power. Still, the USS *Thresher*, the first nuclear submarine to be lost, was the worst submarine disaster in history.

APPENDIX A

Statement announcing the Thresher *is*
"overdue and presumed missing"

NEWS RELEASE
PLEASE NOTE DATE

DEPARTMENT OF DEFENSE
OFFICE OF PUBLIC AFFAIRS
Washington 25, D. C.

8:00 P.M. (EST)
April 10, 1963

NO. 509-63
OXford 76161

Statement by Admiral George W. Anderson, Chief, Naval Operations at the Pentagon, Wednesday, April 10, 1963, 8:00 p.m., on USS THRESHER.

The next of kin of the crew of the nuclear submarine USS THRESHER (SSN-593) are being notified that the ship is overdue and presumed missing.

The THRESHER had been conducting routine tests some 220 miles east of Boston. The submarine rescue vessel USS SKYLARK was accompanying the THRESHER. This procedure is normal for submarine tests and trials following an overhaul.

SKYLARK reported that THRESHER has not communicated as scheduled since beginning deep dive tests shortly after 9 A.M. (EST) this morning.

While there is a possibility that the nuclear submarine has not reported her position due to a communication failure, a search was immediately commenced by the Navy in accordance with emergency proceedings for such situations.

Navy ships, aircraft and other submarines are searching the area where the THRESHER was last reported. They are encountering cloudy weather with winds of from 25 to 40 knots and seas of from 5 to 9 feet. Such conditions would make it difficult for the on-scene search units to sight the overdue submarine even though it were on the surface and unable to transmit a position report by radio communications.

The location of the THRESHER from her last report was given as 41.44 North and 64.57 W. The depth of water at this location is approximately 8400 feet (1400 fathoms). Merchant ships in this area have been requested to keep a sharp lookout for the submarine in addition to the maximum effort being made by the Navy.

Additional reports on the progress of the search will be made by the Navy. Names and addresses of the members of the crew will be released after all next of kin have been notified that the ship is overdue.

END

APPENDIX B

The first press briefing of the Thresher *disaster*

PRESS BRIEFING
BY
ADMIRAL GEORGE W. ANDERSON
CHIEF OF NAVAL OPERATIONS

9:30 P.M.
Wednesday, 10 April, 1963

ADMIRAL ANDERSON: To those of us who have been brought up in the traditions of the sea, one of the saddest occasions is when we lose a ship. Such was the case today when it appears that the nuclear powered submarine THRESHER was lost with 129 officers, men and civilians. The THRESHER had completed an overhaul at the Naval Ship Yard in Portsmouth, New Hampshire, and was undergoing her sea trials. She left the Naval Ship Yard yesterday, did some shallow dives, and today was scheduled to approach her designed test depth, which is of course a classified statistic.

She dove this morning, and has not been heard from since. We are using the full resources of the Navy, surface ships, submarines and aircraft, in an effort to locate the THRESHER if she is still afloat. We are not optimistic at this time, but we are of course hopeful.

QUESTION: Admiral, has the submarine been spotted, located as yet?

ADMIRAL ANDERSON: Not definitely. Late this afternoon just before dark, there was a report that there was an oil slick sighted in the vicinity of the position where the submarine had last dived, but of course we have no definite information.

QUESTION: At that point, Admiral, is a rescue possible?

ADMIRAL ANDERSON: If the submarine sank in the depth of water of 8,400 feet, 1400 fathoms, rescue would be absolutely out of the question.

QUESTION: Admiral, you say it appears that the THRESHER was lost. Is there any real hope that it may yet be found with men alive?

ADMIRAL ANDERSON: There is always the possibility that there has been some communication failure, and that the ship, being unable to communicate with the rescue vessel which was in the vicinity, and perhaps having lost it in the conditions at sea, it is proceeding to port, and that we would hear from her later on. This is our fervent hope, but as I say, we cannot be overly optimistic.

QUESTION: Can you say whether the THRESHER was trying to dive to its maximum test depth when it was last heard from?

ADMIRAL ANDERSON: That was the purpose of this particular test.

QUESTION: Admiral, is there any chance that there was a nuclear explosion in the submarine?

ADMIRAL ANDERSON: I would say that there is absolutely no chance of a nuclear explosion in the submarine, nor is there any likelihood that there would be any radioactive contamination or any danger to navigation resulting from the nuclear reactor being involved in this type of accident.

QUESTION: Admiral, in a situation such as this, if the men are still alive and trapped below, for how long might they survive?

ADMIRAL ANDERSON: If this submarine sank in water of that depth in which she was operating, I would say that there would be absolutely no possibility that they would still be alive. The hope is that the submarine did not sink, but is proceeding out of communication back to port.

QUESTION: Do you have any theory, Admiral, as to what might have happened?

ADMIRAL ANDERSON: No. We have appointed a court of inquiry headed by one of our senior admirals, Vice Admiral Austin, the President of the Naval War College, assisted by other experienced submarine officers, to conduct an inquiry. I would not presume to judge what might have happened in this case.

QUESTION: Has there been any previous structural trouble with this class of submarine?

ADMIRAL ANDERSON: Not at all.

QUESTION: Has there been any difficulty of any kind with any nuclear powered submarine that might have led to something like this?

ADMIRAL ANDERSON: Not to my knowledge, and I am sure that I would have heard of it if there were.

QUESTION: Admiral, what ships do you have in the area and where did they come from, what kinds of ships and how many?

ADMIRAL ANDERSON: We have in the area submarine rescue vessels, particularly the one that was present with the THRESHER when she dove, the SKYLARK, another submarine rescue vessel, the RECOVERY. We have destroyers en route and we have had the area covered by patrol planes throughout the afternoon, and tonight.

QUESTION: What is the purpose of the destroyers? They would not be used in any rescue, would they?

ADMIRAL ANDERSON: No, but to search the area in the event that the submarine were proceeding on the surface and out of communication.

QUESTION: Admiral, do you plan to go to the scene yourself?

ADMIRAL ANDERSON: No, I do not. We have on the scene Admiral Lawson P. Ramage, the Deputy Commander of Submarines, Atlantic Fleet, a very experienced submarine officer, Congressional Medal of Honor winner of World War II in submarines, who is in direct charge of the operations.

QUESTION: Admiral, could you go over very briefly the history as you see it, as you understand it, of this tragedy?

ADMIRAL ANDERSON: Well, this submarine was the first of a new class submarine, the finest submarines in the world we believe, the deepest diving and among the fastest submarines in the world. She was built at the Naval Ship Yard in Portsmouth, launched on July 9, 1960, commissioned on August 3, of 1961. Throughout 1961 and the early part of 1962, the submarine operated in various tests, operations with the fleet and in July of 1962 went into Portsmouth for overhaul and incorporation of new electronic equipment and modernization, so to speak. She just completed that overhaul and was undergoing the tests which we normally give to any ship on completion of an overhaul, to make sure that she is ready for sea and service with the fleet. She conducted shallow dives yesterday and today was scheduled to conduct test dives.

QUESTION: Can you tell us anything more about what happened today, sir?

ADMIRAL ANDERSON: No, other than the fact that she started the day's work on schedule this morning, and the last communication with the submarine was in mid-morning.

QUESTION: Is it possible that sabotage might have figured in this accident?

ADMIRAL ANDERSON: I would say that is probably a remote possibility, but something that the court of inquiry would certainly have to consider.

QUESTION: Admiral Anderson, has there ever been a worse submarine disater, assuming this one is lost?

ADMIRAL ANDERSON: The last submarine disaster that we had in peace time where there was loss of the submarine and loss of life was in 1939, in the case of the U.S.S. SQUALUS. She sank on the 23rd of May 1939 in 40 fathoms of water off Wight Island and the Isle of Shoals off the New Hampshire coast. Of the 59 men aboard, 33 were rescued, and there were 26 casualties. The submarine was subsequently raised, renamed, and saw action in World War II.

Now, of course, during World War II we lost many submarines with large numbers of our fine submarine personnel aboard. The French and other nations have also lost submarines. This is part of the penalty that we pay for the progress that we make in developing these fine naval forces and submarine forces which we have to have in these days.

QUESTION: Admiral, if it was realized that say ten or eleven o'clock or noon this morning that something was amiss, what is the sequence of events that took it so long for us to learn about it?

ADMIRAL ANDERSON: The only reason that we did not make it public prior to the time we did this evening was that first of all, we did not want to unnecessarily alarm the families of the personnel who are aboard, and particularly so because we were in a phase where we were examining to the best of our ability whether or not it was simply a case of communication failure. As that prospect diminished, we felt the responsibility to make the possibility of this serious accident known as soon as we could after the personnel's families had been notified.

QUESTION: Is a submarine normally completely out of communication when it dives to its maximum depth?

ADMIRAL ANDERSON: This depends to a very large degree on the sea conditions which prevail, particularly the temperature conditions in the water. Communication through the water is a very difficult proposition, and was a factor in this case, at least we considered it was a potential factor in the case.

QUESTION: Admiral, if the sub is on the bottom at that depth, is there any possibility of getting back any parts of it?

ADMIRAL ANDERSON: No, there is no possibility of getting any part of it back. We are of course considering the possibility of using the deep diving experimental submarine TRIESTE, which the Navy has on the west coast, to see if we could locate the submarine and thereby perhaps ascertain whether or what was the cause of the accident. But this is a matter which we will have to consider in the future, because it would not involve saving any lives.

QUESTION: Admiral, at what hour did you start your search and rescue work today?

ADMIRAL ANDERSON: The search was developed intensively early this afternoon.

QUESTION: Admiral, could you tell us whether this will cause you to reconsider the construction of future submarines of this class?

ADMIRAL ANDERSON: Not at all. There is no alternative to us proceeding as we are in developing these submarines. We will of course examine all the technical features which we can to make sure that our submarines in the future are as safe as we have had this record in the past. This is a setback, if it is indeed an accident, but we will overcome it as we have others.

THE PRESS: Thank you very much, Admiral Anderson.
The Death of the U.S.S. THRESHER

APPENDIX C

"Death certificate" for the 129 Navymen and civilians aboard the Thresher *on April 10, 1963*

NAVAL MESSAGE
OPNAV FORM 2110-28 (REV. 3-61)

RELEASED BY		DRAFTED BY			PHONE EXT. NR.		PAGE	PAGES
H. L. JENKINS		J. M. YOUNG Pers-G2a			42772			
DATE	TOR/TOD		ROUTED BY		CHECKED BY		OF	
12 April 1962								

MESSAGE NR	DATE/TIME GROUP (GCT)	PRECE-DENCE	FLASH	EMERGENCY	OPERATIONAL IMMEDIATE	PRIORITY	ROUTINE	DEFERRED
	121935Z	ACTION				X		
		INFO				X		

FROM: BUPERS

TO: COMSUBDEV GROUP TWO

INFO: SECNAV · · · COM TWELVE · · · NAVSHIPYD PORTSMOUTH
CNO · · · COM THIRTEEN · · · NAVFINCEN CLEVE
CINCLANTFLT · · · COM FOURTEEN · · · FAMALACT CLEVE
COM ONE · · · COM FIFTEEN · · · OIR
COM THREE · · · COM SEVENTEEN
COM FOUR · · · BUMED
COM FIVE · · · JAG
COM SIX · · · COMSUBLANT
COM EIGHT · · · COMSUBPAC
COM NINE · · · DEPCOMSUBLANT
COM TEN · · · NAVCOMPT
COM ELEVEN · · · SUB BASE NEW LONDON

UNCLAS

1. DETERMINATION MADE AT 2000 ON 11 APRIL 1963, UNDER THE MISSING PERSONS ACT, 50 APP USCA 1005, THAT ALL PERSONNEL ABOARD THE USS THRESHER ON 10 APRIL 1963 DIED ON 10 APRIL 1963.

APPENDIX D

Report of the Thresher *Court of Inquiry*

NEWS RELEASE
PLEASE NOTE DATE

DEPARTMENT OF DEFENSE
OFFICE OF PUBLIC AFFAIRS
Washington 25, D. C.

No. 885-63

IMMEDIATE RELEASE   JUNE 20, 1963   OXford 76161

THRESHER COURT OF INQUIRY REPORTS

A flooding casualty in the engine room is believed to be the "most probable" cause of the sinking of the nuclear submarine USS THRESHER, lost April 10, 1963, 220 miles east of Cape Cod with 129 persons aboard.

The Navy believes it most likely that a piping system failure had occurred in one of the THRESHER's salt water systems, probably in the engine room. The enormous pressure of sea water surrounding the submarine subjected her interior to a violent spray of water and progressive flooding. In all probability water affected electrical circuits and caused loss of power. THRESHER slowed and began to sink. Within moments she had exceeded her collapse depth and totally flooded. She came to rest on the ocean floor, 8,400 feet beneath the surface.

This opinion of the Court of Inquiry was made public today by Secretary of the Navy Fred Korth.

The Court, headed by Vice Admiral Bernard L. Austin, USN, heard testimony from 120 witnesses, both military and civilian, during the eight weeks it was in session at the Naval Shipyard, Portsmouth, New Hampshire. It recorded 1700 pages of testimony and gathered for the record some 255 charts, drawings, letters, photographs, directives, debris and other exhibits bearing on the sinking.

The Record of Proceedings of the Court was delivered last week to the convening authority, Admiral H. Page Smith, USN, Commander-in-Chief, U.S. Atlantic Fleet, who transmitted it, with his comments, to the Secretary of the Navy. Copies of the bulky 12-volume record are now being studied in the Navy Department by engineers, designers and experts in nuclear submarine operations.

The Court declared that, in its opinion, "the basic design of the THRESHER class submarine is good, and its implementation has resulted in the development of a high-performance submarine."

The bulk of the Court's recommendations stated the need for careful review of the design, construction and inspection of vital submarine systems, such as sea water and air systems, and a review of operating procedures to improve damage control capability under casualty conditions such as flooding.

Certain actions have already been taken. For example, the Navy's Bureau of Ships is applying a newly developed inspection technique to assure the integrity of high pressure piping systems on all naval ships. Based upon ultrasonic principles, the new method is being employed initially on nuclear submarines. Personnel training and ultrasonic inspection equipment familiarization are necessary and some rescheduling of submarine construction dates and overhaul intervals will be required. (More)

Much of the testimony heard by the Court was received in closed session and its overall report is classified "secret" to prevent disclosure of the capabilities of the Navy's nuclear submarine force. Secretary Korth has authorized the release of the following portions of the record which do not contain secret information:

Among its opinions, the Court stated that "the evidence does not establish that the deaths of those embarked in THRESHER were caused by the intent, fault, negligence or inefficiency of any person or persons in the naval service or connected therewith."

The Court also reported there was no evidence of sabotage or hostile action in connection with the loss of THRESHER. In addition, the Court found that there was no indication of increased radioactivity in the search area. Debris recovered was also found to be free of radioactive material.

The record states that it is impossible, with the information now available, to obtain a more precise determination of what actually happened.

The Court did, however, offer a "reasonable rationalization of probable events" which, when pieced together with known facts, provide the following chronology of the death of the THRESHER:

The THRESHER, under command of Lieutenant Commander John W. Harvey, USN, departed Portsmouth Naval Shipyard on the morning of April 9, 1963, to conduct scheduled sea trials following an overhaul period which extended from July 16, 1962, to April 11, 1963. THRESHER was a unit of Submarine Development Group TWO and was operating under the orders of Commander, Submarine Force, U.S. Atlantic Fleet (Administration) Portsmouth, for the sea trials. One hundred twenty-nine persons were aboard THRESHER for the purpose of executing official duties. Included in this number were three officers and 13 civilian employees of the Portsmouth Naval Shipyard; one officer from the staff of the Deputy Commander, Submarine Force, Atlantic Fleet; four civilian contractor's representatives, and 12 officers and 96 enlisted men of the ship's company.

USS SKYLARK, commanded by Lieutenant Commander Stanley Hecker, USN, was designated to act as escort to THRESHER during sea trials and effected a rendezvous with the submarine at 9:49 A.M. on April 9 in the vicinity of Latitude 42-56 North, Longitude 70-26 West. Upon completion of a scheduled shallow dive, the two ships proceeded independently during the night to a second rendezvous in the vicinity of Latitude 41-46 North, Longitude 65-03 West. During this transit, THRESHER proceeded both submerged and surfaced and conducted various test evolutions, including full power propulsion.

At 7:45 A.M. on April 10, the two ships were at the rendezvous point, separated by a distance of 3,400 yards. The sea was calm with a slight swell. Wind was from the north-northeast at seven knots. Visibility was about 10 miles. No other ships are known to have been in the vicinity.

Two minutes later, at 7:47 A.M., THRESHER reported by underwater telephone that she was starting a deep dive. SKYLARK maintained her approximate position while THRESHER reported course and depth changes as she

2   (More)

maneuvered beneath the surface. To personnel aboard SKYLARK, the dive appeared to be progressing satisfactorily until about 9:13 A.M., when THRESHER reported "Experiencing minor difficulties. Have positive up angle. Am attempting to blow. Will keep you informed."

Listeners aboard SKYLARK next heard sounds of compressed air rushing into the submarine's ballast tanks as THRESHER sought to regain the surface.

Three minutes later, at about 9:16 A.M., SKYLARK heard a garbled transmission which was believed to contain the words "....test depth."

Upon receiving THRESHER's message that she was experiencing minor difficulty, her escort ship SKYLARK advised THRESHER that the area was clear. She announced her own course and requested range and bearings from the submarine. At about 9:15 A.M., SKYLARK asked THRESHER "Are you in control?" and repeated this query. At 9:21 A.M., SKYLARK established her position by Loran as Latitude 41-45 North, Longitude 64-59 West. She continued her attempts to communicate with THRESHER by underwater telephone, sonar and radio. Then, at 10:40 A.M., SKYLARK commenced dropping a series of hand grenades as a signal to THRESHER that she should surface. SKYLARK then sent a message to Commander Submarine Development Group TWO reporting that she had lost contact with the submarine.

The Court of Inquiry concluded that the SKYLARK's message "did not convey to operational commanders the full extent of the information available." Lieutenant Commander Hecker was named a party to the investigation but, in the opinion of the Court, SKYLARK's actions "could not conceivably have contributed in any way to the loss of THRESHER..."

"The tragic loss of THRESHER has caused the Navy to review in minute detail the design, construction, operation and overhaul of our nuclear submarines," Secretary Korth said. "We have found nothing to cast doubt on the basic soundness of the program, but in every analysis of a major catastrophe at sea, lessons are learned. The Record of Proceedings of the Court of Inquiry headed by Vice Admiral Austin is receiving most careful and detailed scrutiny. It will undoubtedly serve to lessen the hazards inherent in operating beneath the sea."

END

APPENDIX E

Statement announcing the finding of the Thresher's remains

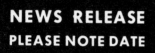 **NEWS RELEASE**
PLEASE NOTE DATE

DEPARTMENT OF DEFENSE
OFFICE OF PUBLIC AFFAIRS
Washington 25, D. C.

IMMEDIATE RELEASE   September 5, 1963   NO. 1207-63
OXFORD 76161

STATEMENT OF SECRETARY OF THE NAVY FRED KORTH
ON 5-MONTH LONG SEARCH FOR SUBMARINE THRESHER

The location of structural parts of the THRESHER on the ocean floor having been positively confirmed by the bathyscaph TRIESTE during her latest series of successful dives, I have today directed that the associated operational aspects of the search for the nuclear submarine THRESHER be terminated.

The latest series of five dives by the TRIESTE have been tremendously successful. In her third dive, on August 24, 1963, the bathyscaph took a number of extremely valuable photographs and made a unique recovery from the ocean floor. The item recovered was a length of copper piping and a fitting with markings which definitely established that it came from THRESHER. The piping was picked up by a mechanical arm operated from inside TRIESTE's gondola in the first successful test of this device.

More than three dozen ships and thousands of men have been engaged for nearly five months in detailed probings of the ocean floor where the THRESHER lies in 8,400 feet of water. These efforts, combined with the evidence gathered by TRIESTE during the latest series of dives, have produced conclusive information that we know the general area where the THRESHER lies. We are equally sure that she poses no hazard, even to marine life. Thus, having successfully completed the search phase, we are encouraged that we can now proceed with that phase of further exploration which will be directed toward obtaining more precise and valuable scientific information about the THRESHER area.

The five dives just completed by TRIESTE bring to a total of 10 the number of times she has explored the ocean floor in search of the sunken submarine. She carried out an earlier series of dives in June and July after being brought from the West Coast to join the search force. As previously announced, TRIESTE and her supporting ships, the salvage ship USS PRESERVER and the landing ship dock USS FORT SNELLING, returned to Boston yesterday after 17 days on station. Observers aboard the bathyscaph have both seen and photographed a large amount of debris on the ocean floor, much of it directly correlated to THRESHER.

In Boston, TRIESTE will undergo a detailed inspection to determine the extent of the work required to refit her for further undersea explorations. The exact extent and timing of this work cannot be determined until the scheduled inspection is completed. After this inspection and the review of the work schedule, a determination will be made as to whether the TRIESTE will be held in the Boston area or returned to her home station, the Naval Electronics Laboratory in San Diego.

MORE

In view of the rapidly deteriorating weather conditions in the THRESHER search area this fall, we may not be able to finish the work on TRIESTE in time to use her again this year for the scientific program, despite the intense desires by many to continue to explore in the area where the recent photographs were taken.

Although TRIESTE may not be available, the exploration work in the THRESHER area will continue as an integral part of the Navy's research and development program. The limited state-of-the-art of underwater reconnaissance has imposed severe restrictions on this effort to date, but these restrictions have served only to motivate and excite those many dedicated people engaged in the search. Tremendously valuable information has been developed. Compared with what many knowledgeable people predicted at the time that we started, the results have been outstanding. For example, one must recall that the TRIESTE was not designed for tasks such as those that she has recently completed.

Encouraged by the results to date and with the expectations of gaining further detailed information from those heretofore unexplored depths of the ocean, we are planning to continue with the exploration work in the THRESHER area. As a part of this effort, periodic surveys will be made in the area using oceanographic research ships and new deep submergence vehicles and systems as they are developed. This program will be directed by the Chief of Naval Research, Rear Admiral Leonidas D. Coates, Jr., USN. He will be working in conjunction with the Oceanographer of the Navy, Rear Admiral Denys W. Knoll, USN. They will be assisted by members of the Deep Submergence Systems Review Group headed by Rear Admiral Edward C. Stephan, USN (Retired.)

Much of the burden of the five-month search fell largely to four oceanographic research ships, the Military Sea Transportation Service ships GILLISS and GIBBS; the Lamont Geological Observatory ship CONRAD, and the Woods Hole Oceanographic Institution vessel ATLANTIS II. Using deep-towed still and television cameras, magnetometers and sonars, the ships made exhaustive electronic probes of the bottom and took thousands of photographs. As a result, the area of the search is now better known to oceanographers than any area of similar depth anywhere in the world.

Since the outset, the search operation has been under the operational control of Admiral I. P. Smith, USN, Commander in Chief, U. S. Atlantic Fleet. The on-the-scene commander has been Captain Frank A. Andrews, USN, Commander of Submarine Development Group TWO, the group to which THRESHER was assigned at the time of her loss. Dr. Arthur Maxwell of the Office of Naval Research has served as Chairman of the Technical Advisory Group, an organization of scientists and experts in submarine operations which has functioned as a "steering committee" during search operations.

The bathyscaph TRIESTE is under command of Lieutenant Commander Donald Keach, USN.

These gentlemen are with me today and together we will be glad to reply to any questions you may have.

END

APPENDIX F

The 129 Navymen and civilians who died in the Thresher

Officers of the *Thresher*

LIEUTENANT (JUNIOR GRADE) RONALD C. BABCOCK (Communications, Sonar and Electronics Officer)

LIEUTENANT MERRILL F. COLLIER

*LIEUTENANT COMMANDER MICHAEL J. DI NOLA (Main Propulsion Assistant)

*LIEUTENANT COMMANDER PAT M. GARNER (Executive Officer)

LIEUTENANT (JUNIOR GRADE) JOHN G. GRAFTON

*LIEUTENANT COMMANDER JOHN W. HARVEY (Commanding Officer)

LIEUTENANT (JUNIOR GRADE) JAMES J. HENRY JR. (Supply and Commissary Officer)

**LIEUTENANT COMMANDER JOHN S. LYMAN JR. (Engineer Officer)

LIEUTENANT (JUNIOR GRADE) FRANK J. MALINSKI

LIEUTENANT (JUNIOR GRADE) GUY C. PARSONS JR. (First Lieutenant, Torpedo and Gunnery Officer)

**LIEUTENANT JOHN SMARZ JR. (Damage Control Assistant and "A" Division Officer)

LIEUTENANT (JUNIOR GRADE) JOHN J. WILEY

Officer Observers

*LIEUTENANT COMMANDER PHILIP H. ALLEN (Staff, Portsmouth Naval Shipyard)

**LIEUTENANT ROBERT D. BIEDERMAN (Staff, Portsmouth Naval Shipyard)

*LIEUTENANT COMMANDER JOHN H. BILLINGS (Staff, Portsmouth Naval Shipyard)

**LIEUTENANT COMMANDER ROBERT L. KRAG (Staff, Deputy Commander, Submarine Force Atlantic)

Civilian Observers

FRED P. AMBRAMS, Portsmouth Naval Shipyard
DANIEL W. BEAL JR.,Portsmouth Naval Shipyard
ROBERT E. CHARRON, Portsmouth Naval Shipyard
K. R. CORCORAN, Sperry Gyroscope Company
KENNETH J. CRITCHLEY, Portsmouth Naval Shipyard
PAUL C. CURRIER, Portsmouth Naval Shipyard
RICHARD R. DES JARDINS, Portsmouth Naval Shipyard
GEORGE J. DINEEN, Portsmouth Naval Shipyard
RICHARD K. FISHER, Portsmouth Naval Shipyard
PAUL A. GUERETTE, Portsmouth Naval Shipyard
MAURICE F. JAQUAY, Raytheon Company
D. KUESTER, Naval Ordnance Laboratory
HENRY MOREAU, Portsmouth Naval Shipyard
FRANKLIN J. PALMER, Portsmouth Naval Shipyard
ROBERT D. PRESCOTT, Portsmouth Naval Shipyard
D. STADTMULLER, Sperry Gyroscope Company
LAURENCE WHITTEN, Portsmouth Naval Shipyard

Enlisted Men

ARSENAULT, TILMON J., Chief Engineman
BAIN, RONALD E., Engineman 2/c
BELL, JOHN E., Machinist's Mate 1/c
BOBBITT, EDGAR S., Electrician's Mate 2/c
†BOSTER, GERALD C., Electrician's Mate 3/c
BRACEY, GEORGE, Steward 3/c
BRANN, RICHARD P., Engineman 2/c
†CARKOSKI, RICHARD J., Engineman 2/c
CARMODY, PATRICK W., Storekeeper 2/c
CAYEY, STEVEN G., Torpedoman's Mate 2/c
†CHRISTIANSEN, EDWARD, Seaman
CLAUSSEN, LARRY W., Electrician's Mate 2/c
CLEMENTS, THOMAS E., Electronics Technician 3/c
CUMMINGS, FRANCIS M., Sonarman 2/c
†DABRUZZI, SAMUEL J., Electronics Technician 2/c
DAVISON, CLYDE E., III, Electronics Technician 3/c
DAY, DONALD C., Engineman 3/c

DENNY, ROY O., JR., Electrician's Mate 1/c
DI BELLA, PETER J., Seaman
DUNDAS, DON R., Electronics Technician 2/c
DYER, TROY E., Electronics Technician 1/c
FOTI, RAYMOND P., Electronics Technician 1/c
FORNI, ELLWOOD H., Chief Sonarman
FREEMAN, LARRY W., Fire Control Technician 2/c
FUSCO, GREGORY J., Electrician's Mate 2/c
GALLANT, ANDREW J., JR., Chief Hospital Corpsman
GARCIA, NAPOLEON T., Steward 1/c
GARNER, JOHN E., Yeoman Seaman
GAYNOR, ROBERT W., Engineman 2/c
GOSNELL, ROBERT H., Seaman Apprentice
GRAHAM, WILLIAM E., Chief Sonarman
†GUNTER, AARON J., Quartermaster 1/c
HALL, RICHARD C., Electronics Technician 2/c
HAYES, NORMAN T., Electrician's Mate 1/c
HEISER, LAIRD G., Machinist's Mate 1/c
HELSIUS, MARVIN T., Machinist's Mate 2/c
HEWITT, LEONARD H., Chief Electrician's Mate
†HOAGUE, JOSEPH H., Torpedoman's Mate 2/c
HODGE, JAMES P., Electrician's Mate 2/c
†HUDSON, JOHN F., Engineman 2/c
INGLIS, JOHN P., Fireman
JOHNSON, BRAWNER G., Fire Control Technician 1/c
JOHNSON, EDWARD A., Chief Engineman
JOHNSON, RICHARD L., Radioman Seaman Apprentice
JOHNSON, ROBERT E., Chief Torpedoman's Mate
JOHNSON, THOMAS B., Electronics Technician 1/c
JONES, RICHARD W., Electrician's Mate 2/c
KALUZA, EDMUND J., JR., Sonarman 2/c
KANTZ, THOMAS C., Electronics Technician 2/c
†KEILER, RONALD D., Interior Communications Electrician 2/c
KEARNEY, ROBERT D., Machinist's Mate 3/c
KIESECKER, GEORGE J., Machinist's Mate 2/c
KLIER, BILLY M., Engineman 1/c
KRONER, GEORGE R., Commissaryman 3/c
LANQUETTE, NORMAN G., Quartermaster 1/c
LAVOIE, WAYNE W., Yeoman 1/c
MABRY, TEMPLEMAN N., JR., Engineman 2/c

†MANN, RICHARD H., JR., Interior Communications Electrician 2/c
MARULLO, JULIUS F., JR., Quartermaster 1/c
MCCLELLAND, DOUGLAS R., Electrician's Mate 3/c
MCCORD, DONALD J., Machinist's Mate 1/c
MCDONOUGH, KARL P., Torpedoman's Mate 3/c
MIDDLETON, SIDNEY L., Machinist's Mate 1/c
MUISE, RONALD A., Commissaryman 2/c
MUSSELWHITE, JAMES A., Electronics Technician 2/c
NAULT, DONALD E., Commissaryman 1/c
NOONIS, WALTER J., Chief Radioman
NORRIS, JOHN D., Electronics Technician 1/c
OETTING, CHESLEY C., Electrician's Mate 2/c
PENNINGTON, ROSCOE C., Chief Electrician's Mate
PETERS, JAMES G., Senior Electrician's Mate
PHILLIPPI, JAMES F., Sonarman 2/c
PHILPUT, DAN A., Engineman 2/c
PODWELL, RICHARD, Machinist's Mate 2/c
REGAN, JOHN S., Machinist's Mate 1/c
RITCHIE, JAMES P., Radioman 2/c
ROUNTREE, GLENN A., Quartermaster 2/c
ROBISON, PERVIS, Seaman
RUSHETSKI, ANTHONY A., Electronics Technician 2/c
SCHIEWE, JAMES M., Electrician's Mate 1/c
SHAFER, BENJAMIN N., Master Chief Electrician's Mate
SHAFER, JOHN D., Senior Chief Electrician's Mate
SHIMKO, JOSEPH T., Machinist's Mate 1/c
†SHOTWELL, BURNETT M., Electronics Technician Seaman
SINNETT, ALAN D., Fire Control Technician 2/c
SMITH, WILLIAM H., JR., Boilerman 1/c
SNIDER, JAMES L., Machinist's Mate 1/c
†SOLOMON, RONALD H., Electrician's Mate 1/c
STEINEL, ROBERT E., Sonarman 1/c
VAN PELT, ROGER E., Interior Communications Electrician 1/c
WALSKI, JOSEPH A., Radioman 1/c
WASEL, DAVID A., Radioman Seaman
WIGGINS, CHARLES L., Fire Control Technician 1/c
WISE, DONALD E., Chief Machinist's Mate
†WOLFE, RONALD E., Quartermaster Seaman
ZWEIFEL, JAY H., Electrician's Mate 2/c

* Qualified for Command of Submarines.
** Qualified in Submarines.

Lieutenants Collier, Grafton, Malinski, and Wiley performed a variety of duties, but did not have "division" assignments.

All of the Thresher's officers except Lieutenants Malinski and Smarz were qualified in nuclear propulsion.

† Twelve enlisted men who were lost in the Thresher were posthumously promoted to the next highest grade. The promotions were made effective from April 10 when the submarine was lost. They were awarded to men who normally would have been advanced May 16 or later.